ADVANCE PRAISE

"The Prenup Prescription is a must-read. Aaron compares marriage today to two fully formed corporations that come together as one. How could any such arrangement lead to 'happily ever after' without a contract in place? Aaron provides the actionable education in prenups needed to help a couple engineer their own healthy and successful marriage, one set on a foundation of transparency, communication, and fairness—the key tenets of a healthy relationship. Aaron's insight into the world of family law and prenups is the definition of 'private lives are public issues.'"

—EVE RODSKY, AUTHOR OF THE *NEW YORK TIMES*
BESTSELLER (AND REESE'S BOOK CLUB PICK)
FAIR PLAY AND *FIND YOUR UNICORN SPACE*

"A prenup can do so much more than simply outline how you'll divide assets in the case of divorce. A dynamic premarital contract, like those Aaron 'prescribes,' can actually save your marriage! We've all heard money is the number-one thing couples fight about, so who wouldn't want to know the secret to eliminating those battles and preserving the peace in a mar-

riage? With a mix of relationship advice, legal know-how, and financial blueprints, Aaron guides couples through the clear conversations needed to create a transparent, ongoing plan with regard to all things money. He also shows readers how to truly commit to those plans by integrating them into a prenup. Aaron changed my views on prenups, and in *The Prenup Prescription* he shows you just how valuable a tool they can be."

—MINDY JENSEN, HOST OF *BIGGERPOCKETS MONEY PODCAST* AND CO-AUTHOR OF *FIRST-TIME HOME BUYER: THE COMPLETE PLAYBOOK TO AVOIDING ROOKIE MISTAKES*

"*The Prenup Prescription* should be required reading for every engaged—and married—couple! Aaron explains how a prenup isn't a divorce plan, but it can be a financial relationship plan. He provides invaluable advice for everyone—whether you're still glowing over your shiny new ring or you've been married for decades—about not fighting over money and staying happily married. Genius!"

—STEPHANIE EVERETT, CEO OF LAWYERIST, HOST OF *THE LAWYERIST PODCAST*, AND CO-AUTHOR OF *THE SMALL FIRM ROADMAP*

THE PRENUP PRESCRIPTION

the Prenup Prescription

MEET THE **PREMARITAL CONTRACT** DESIGNED TO SAVE YOUR MARRIAGE

Aaron Thomas

LIONCREST

PUBLISHING

THE PRENUP PRESCRIPTION

Meet the Premarital Contract Designed to Save Your Marriage

FIRST EDITION

ISBN   978-1-5445-3511-1   *Hardcover*

978-1-5445-3510-4   *Paperback*

978-1-5445-3509-8   *Ebook*

Contents

INTRODUCTION...11

PART ONE

1. SO WHAT IS MARRIAGE, LEGALLY SPEAKING? 23
2. THE DREADED D-WORD 33
3. A CRASH COURSE IN PRENUPS 47

PART TWO

4. STEP 1: LAY BARE YOUR CURRENT FINANCES........65
5. STEP TWO: SET UP YOUR ACCOUNTS AND
   SORT YOUR FINANCES..77
6. STEP THREE: PLAN FOR YOUR FUTURE 89
7. TACT, TIMING, AND TALK..111
   CONCLUSION...117

APPENDIX

TIMELINE OF MARRIAGE LAWS...................................123
TIMELINE OF DIVORCE LAWS 133
MARRIAGE ANACHRONISMS 139
A POSTNUP P.S... 143
HOW DIVORCE BECAME NO ONE'S FAULT
(AND WHY IT NEEDS TO STAY THAT WAY).............. 149
SCARE-YOU-STRAIGHT CAUTIONARY TALES.........155

Introduction

CONGRATULATIONS! YOU'RE GETTING MARRIED!

(This is where I engage in the proper amount of enthusiastic but rote small talk about your wedding, your venue, your colors, your theme...)

...All that sounds great, really great. Mmm-hmmm. And how about your vows? The lawyer in me compels the ask. You know, funny thing about vows. Got any idea what you're committing to—legally speaking—when you and your fiancé(e) exchange them?

No? Let me clear it up. By standing in front of everyone, declaring your intentions to be married, and signing your marriage license, sure, you're signing up for happily ever after. You're also accepting state laws regarding the legal status of your finances during and—dare I say it?—after your marriage.

In other words, saying "I do," means you've essentially got a prenup by default. What, you haven't read what amounts to the "state prenup?" Most people don't. I'll give you the gist. It was pretty much written in the 1800s—by a bunch of chauvinists. And it's based on a really, really outdated idea of what marriage is. There have been tweaks here and there in the hundreds of years these laws have been around, but the basic bedrock of state prenups is...creaky at best.

Sweating yet? So was I when I was in your shoes.

WHY I DECIDED MARRIAGE—LEGALLY SPEAKING—WAS EVIL

I was a few years out of law school when I first learned about so-called state prenups. I'd graduated and was scraping by on a public defender's salary. For three years, the defender job kept me safely tucked away from my mountain of school debt; luckily, Harvard would pay the student loans of alumni performing public interest work. No matter how much I loved serving my clients—and I did—I wasn't one of those kids with parents who bought them their first house, and I just couldn't save enough to get ahead financially. About that time, a friend set me up with a big-name family law firm, one that represented a lot of athletes and celebrities. (FYI, "Family law" is simply a gentle way of saying divorce law.) They offered the zeros I asked for, and suddenly, I was a divorce lawyer.

The cases I saw in those early days scared me to death. None of my close friends had gone through a divorce. No one in my immediate family had divorced. (As I write this, my parents just celebrated their fifty-seventh wedding anniversary.) I had no idea what the divorce process was like. And, as I learned more and more on the job, *everything* about the process shocked me.

I didn't know that the average contested divorce lasts a year-plus—easily a year and a half post-COVID—and can drag out for ages thereafter. (A contested divorce is one that goes to litigation because the spouses can't agree, or "settle," on spousal support or how to divide their assets and debts.) What an unbearably long time to go through something that's beyond painful! First, you're at the end of a relationship—the relationship that, at some point, you thought was going to last for the rest of your life. And now your financial future is on the line, the custody of your kids is on the line... On top of that, you have to find a lawyer, and let's be honest, lawyers are categorically expensive.

I also learned that in contested divorce cases, what is normally private is made glaringly public. That includes everything from your sex life to your bank accounts, your assets, your debts, what you've spent money on (and how much), how you do—or don't—pay bills, how you do—or don't—do the laundry. Nothing is off-limits. And, with very few exceptions, every little bit is aired in an open courtroom. Afterward, the transcripts, plus any document submitted to the court, are made part of the public record, and remain so, forever.

If that setup weren't cringe-inducing enough, the only reason all the drama unfolds is to inform how a judge will rule amid the confines of existing laws and precedents. Translated, that means the bulk of a divorce verdict has less to do with who did what to whom or who was more virtuous than the other, and more to do with state marriage laws. Talk about cold. It's no wonder divorce fertilizes so many personal fears, from loss of control to financial insecurity, public embarrassment, and the future of one's children, not to mention a person's role in their lives altogether.

The more I learned about family law it became clear: getting married is the same as binding yourself to a legal contract that most people never read. If you break this contract (i.e., get divorced), it puts fundamental personal decisions—what happens to your money, the amount of time you spend with your kids—in the hands of complete strangers, first those who made the laws, then a judge to whom you are assigned at random. I watched what the process did to those who otherwise were good, everyday people, over and over. That's when I decided there's one surefire way to avoid a messy divorce: never get married.

...AND THEN I MET CHRISTINA

Part of my skepticism surrounding marriage had to do with "The One." (As in, "You'll know when you meet The One.") I didn't buy it. *Surely that's just pheromones*, I argued with myself. *There's no way there is just one person out there for each of us, is there? That has to be just a story we tell ourselves, right?*

After some twenty years of dating—and dating some great people—I still hadn't felt any lightning bolts of certainty. I kept debating, *Is this it? Is this how I'm supposed to feel? I don't think it's supposed to be this hard or confusing.* Nothing I'd felt was enough to sign up for what I newly realized about marital law. Commitment is one thing, I'm all about commitment. But why make it a legal endeavor? For children? You can address kids legally without actually getting married, so why?

And then, Christina.

The night we met, I thought I was doing a friend a favor by taking her out. My take was that I was supposed to tell her about Atlanta and the legal community since she's also a lawyer, and had just moved here from New York. She told me she was two years out of a marriage and looking for a fresh start on all fronts. Somehow it came up that her ex-husband had run up a ton of credit card debt in their relationship, and she was on the hook for it with him, just as much as if she'd generated it herself. I was at peak don't-ever-get-married status, so I chimed in with my then-motto, "Yes! Marriage is the worst!" We bonded over being on the same anti-marriage page. I asked her out again.

We dated, and she...she brought romance alive for me. She didn't play games, like waiting for some requisite amount of time before texting me back. She was super loveable—one of those people who everyone loves. She was smart, she was mature, and she even thought I was funny. She was all the things. (Today, she works at a nonprofit where she helps immigrant children. I mean, come on!) It wasn't long before thoughts like, *I legitimately could see myself growing with this person*, led to, *This is the person I want to spend the rest of my life with*, and next, *She's someone I want to raise children with*, followed by, *I had better lock this up before someone else wises up and moves in on her.* Luckily, she had fallen for me, too.

FOLLOW THE MONEY

And that leads us to this book. After years of being a divorce lawyer for everyone from regular professionals like you (and me) to multi-millionaire celebrities, I saw how innocuous, seemingly one-off fights could corrode a marriage's foundation and ultimately lead a couple not to just divorce, but to divorce in a nasty, vicious, and debilitating way. The root source of the contention was no secret: money. But that's not the whole picture. **When I followed the money, I saw that marriage finances, when organized without *transparency*, *communication*, and *fairness*, inevitably lead to chronic, deep-seeded, far-reaching relationship problems.** Why? Because the financial dynamics in a marriage dictate the personal dynamics of that marriage.

Let me say that again:

The financial dynamics in a marriage dictate
the personal dynamics of that marriage.

And when people enter marriage with a lousy financial dynamic, they build their future on a shoddy foundation. For some reason, we're still following an outdated economic model that might have made sense in the 1950s and 1960s but is disaster-making today. Consider this: back when my parents got married in the 1960s, the average age at which their peers tied the knot was about twenty years old. Student loan debt was a fraction of what it is now. Most single twenty-somethings had one bank account, if any, no credit cards (they'd just been invented), no 401(k), no house, and no mortgage. There might be one car between the two of them. All of this made getting married akin to two people starting a business together from scratch—they were building a small startup of their own.

In the 2020s, however, the typical age of someone entering a first marriage lands somewhere in the mid-thirties. Today, each half of a couple likely has four or five bank accounts, four or five credit cards, a mortgaged home with equity, at least one car each, and a 401(k). (Just as importantly, and maybe even more so, each person also has built up at least a decade of their own financial habits.) Clearly, a couple who gets married today amounts to a merger of two fully formed corporations. Would anyone, anywhere agree to a merger of a corporation they owned without a written agreement, one that they had read closely, one they had a hand in writing? Of course not.

Even if a couple today enters marriage with the average prenup (which is one that *doesn't* address how the couple will organize and operate their everyday finances), they fare little better than those who never sought one at all. Sure, if the plane goes down for spouses with the average prenup, each has a tidy, guaranteed-to-work parachute. But what about you—wouldn't you rather the plane didn't go down at all? And while it's airborne, wouldn't you want a smoother ride? I did.

INTEGRATE YOUR PRENUP IN YOUR EVERYDAY PRACTICES

Lawyers are, by nature and profession, problem solvers. I looked at divorce—I still do—like a puzzle to solve. I'm not a quack; I don't have a crystal ball, and I know there is no guarantee any couple will stay together—not even me and my dream gal. But there are plenty of better ways to enter and build marriages than we do now. And it starts before any wedding guests have gathered.

I settled on this: if two people, before they headed down the aisle, addressed and organized all things monetary, it would do wonders for their marriage.

For clarity, this pair would need to write out in black and white all they had agreed upon. And to power up their promises, they would need to hand those plans to a lawyer who could convert their financial blueprint into a legally binding contract.

There are only two contracts that can supplant one-size-fits-all state marital laws: a prenuptial agreement and a postnuptial agreement. (A postnup is essentially a prenup signed after two people are married.) That's it. From a legal perspective, the two documents are equal in power and reach. I focus on prenups due to their timing. Drawing the lines before a wedding sets up a natural and definitive fresh start. I've done plenty of prenups that I turned into postnups because, for one reason or another, a couple couldn't finalize the details before their ceremony. That said, getting a postnup is better than having no personal marital contract at all. (For more on postnups, see the Appendix.)

I look at a prenup as a multi-dimensional tool. If crafted just so and wielded just right, they can regulate how a couple interacts financially during their marriage. That's because the contracts are capable of far more than most people realize. How so? They can include clauses that dictate actions.

Consider that for a moment. You can create a prenup that includes personalized house rules for financial engagement between you and your spouse. View those house rules as healthy, positive behaviors to adopt for the good of your marriage, and the contract bears no relation to the stereotypical defense-minded tabloid prenup we hear about so often. The kind of marital contract I'm talking about represents a seismic shift; it's created to prevent and solve problems rather than punish. This contract is designed to set a couple up for success from the moment they are married and throughout their marriage. With such a prenup, a couple's marriage plane ride is more likely to be smooth, and, should it not be, they have the security of knowing their parachutes are sound.

AND NOW FOR THE (SECRET) SPECIAL SAUCE

The first prenup I engineered from this mindset—to keep a couple married—was my own. I pulled out every such agreement I'd ever written and copied the clauses I liked best—the stuff that addressed payment of expenses during the marriage, the stuff about undergoing arbitration instead of entering the courtroom, and so on. I only put in things that would either make our pending marriage better or, if it came to it, make its dissolution less horrible. (Christina added her own two cents, of course.)

As I worked on it, something became obvious. **The same things that make for a good prenup also make for a good marriage.** I kept coming back to the same three principles that were missing in my clients' marriages: *transparency, communication*, and *fairness*. Each principle is critical to drafting a solid, enforceable prenup. And each principle is critical to a successful marriage.

A typical prenup covers the basics and maybe includes a behavior here (like spending caps) or there. But a prescribed prenup? That's one uniquely designed to help you and your fiancé(e) stay together. That's *The Prenup Prescription*. In the rest of this book, I lay out three steps for you and your partner to undertake; steps that, when worked accordingly, will yield the blueprint for your financial relationship and strengthen the primary tools you need for the healthiest of marriages. When you've completed the steps, you'll take your blueprint to a family law attorney who will then convert it into a legal prenup.

Work *The Prenup Prescription*, and you'll commit to "your person" in an intentional way that suits modern couples far, far better than a simple "I do." And you—both of you—will reap rewards that last far, far longer than any memory of those wedding cake flavors.

Ready? Great. The first stop is a quick immersion course in marriage law. Buckle up for a wild ride; you won't believe how crazy the history is, nor how recently some of the most egregious, most outdated laws have been overturned.

....

Part One

....

CHAPTER ONE

So What Is Marriage, Legally Speaking?

marriage: (n) the legal relationship of two people who are married to one another.

Source: Oxford Learner's Dictionary

AS A LAWYER, I AM COMPELLED TO ELABORATE ON THIS definition of marriage. If I could rewrite it, I would—along with just about every other dictionary's nearly identical verbiage. Here's my alternative: a marriage is a legally recognized union of two people that gives each party rights to the other party's finances, and can also make each responsible for the other's debts and living expenses. How's that for a splash of Arctic-level cold water? It's jarring because engaged people are citizens of two worlds, one of which is not even remotely on their radar. Affianced couples are inundated daily with romantic expectations à la social media, advertising, rom-coms—we know that. But these poor souls are also about to be at the mercy of laws informed by archaic notions that are anything *but* romantic.

Our idea of a romantic marriage, one centered on uniting two loving, equal individuals for a lifelong relationship, has been around for about fifty years. Fifty years. In fact, for 99 percent of recorded history, marital unions were perceived as a transfer of property rights from one owner to another. What's the property? Why, women, of course. And, because, like the Bard himself wrote, "Past is prologue," to understand the institution as it's seen by lawyers and judges, you've got to shine a light backward, one so bright it illuminates the origins of marital law.

Historically speaking, a woman was her father's property until he brokered a marriage with another man. After that, she became her husband's property. Century after century, such "transactions" served several purposes. For example, they might have formed alliances between families, tribes, countries, and on; ensured the legitimacy of a man's children in order to preserve his bloodline; and/or controlled the integrity of one's patriarchal inheritance.

During the eons this paradigm was in place, women were viewed as vessels that produced offspring. In exchange for a wife's fidelity, the husband was expected to feed, clothe, and shelter her and the children their union generated. Rarely, if at all, were there provisions protecting how he should care for her or their kids, and there certainly was no expectation of love or fidelity. Most significantly, there were no escape clauses for the woman.

Should a wife—for whatever reason—be barren or be unable to birth a viable infant, she was in violation of the marriage contract. Breaking that contract meant she would most likely be tossed aside and replaced. And because a respectable man would not be interested in used and/or substandard "goods," an abandoned woman would either return to her parent's home, turn to prostitution, or, perhaps, both.

As foreign as this history may seem now, women as property and marriage as a transaction of said property is an archetype that has been baked into our legal systems and cultures. What, precisely, that means for you today is that the marriage laws surrounding your pending union are based on laws established centuries ago. (You can actually trace them back to the marriage edicts of early America, edicts which were riffs off the British laws that first governed colonial settlers. Those British laws? They were based on English Common Law, which dates back to 1006 AD. In other words, the foundation for every state's marriage laws is old. Really, really old. Middle Ages-old.)[1]

Further, since 1776, antiquated laws only evolve or get dismantled and replaced with newer laws and rulings if American politicians are so inclined, or if the Supreme Court comes to an alternate interpretation of our Constitution and its Amendments. (Hmmm. That sounds especially familiar of late...) Picture who initially served in—and still dominate—local, state, and federal political bodies, and who have, quite literally, "manned" the Supreme Court since it was created: men, and, to be precise, white men.

It's worth thinking about when you're on the precipice of your Big Day, because traditional mores have long favored men, and men have long written marriage laws. In other words, men operating from their inevitably male perspective have shaped—and continue to shape—everything that governs a woman's life. None of this is intended as political fodder. I'm merely stating facts. **My point is that it is critical, especially as a woman, or as a man who supports modern rights for women, that you take a look at the binding marriage laws that take effect the moment you sign a marriage license.**

---

1   For a timeline featuring some of the most shocking laws surrounding marriage and divorce, check out the Appendix.

Whew! This is a lot of heavy talk for the altar-bound, especially for those who would probably prefer to book their bachelor(ette) weekend over a history lesson and reality check. I wish I could say I am sorry, but I'm not. I'm a family law attorney, and one with three sisters, a daughter, and a wife who was married once before. It's my mission to set you and your intended up for success, and to do so, it's essential you know what your prenup will replace—laws governing the dissolution of a marriage.

WHAT'S A CONTRACT SOCIETY (AND WHY DOES IT MATTER)?

A prenuptial agreement is, at its heart, a contract like any other contract. And, as I said in the opening of this book, when you trade marriage vows with someone and sign a legal marriage license, and you *don't* have a prenup in place, you are, by default, agreeing to state laws governing marriage dissolution if and when your marriage breaks up.[2] Laws, which, most likely, you've never read.

---

2   Where you got married and/or where your marriage license was issued is—typically—irrelevant to determining which state's marital laws govern your divorce. What matters most is the state in which the non-filing, "defendant" spouse has established residency at the time they are served divorce papers. You read that correctly: jurisdiction in a divorce is based on the state in which the party who has not initiated divorce proceedings is a legally recognized resident.

All but three states have time requirements to meet before a defendant spouse can claim residency, and thus, be subject to their divorce laws. The forty-seven with stipulations demand a person lives within state lines anywhere from sixty days (Kansas) to a year (South Carolina) before they are considered its legal resident.

 Because state divorce laws vary vastly, I've seen many a case in which the non-filing party moved to another state specifically to benefit from its jurisdiction. These relocators pack their bags and give their spouses a "Bye, Felicia" only to head across state lines, sign a lease, and cross their fingers that their other half doesn't file before they can meet their new home's residency provisions. In Florida, if a couple has been married seventeen years, one party is entitled to a lifetime of alimony. But Georgia alimony? It's up in the air. Which state is the most advantageous—or disadvantageous—for you depends on your marriage and what you stand to gain...or lose. So just get a prenup, already! Doing so takes the guesswork out of your fate. And there already are enough gambles in life without getting forced into a game of musical chairs, divorce jurisdiction edition.

It's not unusual for anyone to be in the dark over legal fine print. Who reads the myriad contracts we enter into and live under daily? Not me, and I'm a lawyer. Usually, it doesn't matter. But what does matter is that anyone living in a contract-based society knows that when they sign a contract, each party can rely on that contract being enforceable by law.

Say you're on vacation, and you rent a scooter. The scooter owner tells you their rental contract says if you're late with your return, you'll be charged fifty bucks. In reality, the chance you'll get dragged into court over such a small sum is slim, very slim. But how many late-return customers pay the fifty dollars? Pretty much everyone. That's because America is a contract-based society, which means here, when we sign something like a rental contract, we accept that we have consented to its terms and that we are bound by those terms—regardless if we've read them or not. The true power of a scooter rental contract stems from a society's adherence to contracts, deference to contracts, and innate acceptance of a legal system that upholds contracts.

Here's why that's important for those on the way to a wedding: in a country built on contract adherence, judges and their ilk give strong, strong, strong preference to enforcing a signed contract—even if its terms are not seen as fair. In fact, they tend to enforce a contract *especially* when its terms are not seen as fair.

Why would they do such a seemingly illogical thing? Because our society is held together by the legal glue of contracts. People stake billions of dollars on the belief that their investments are, by law, protected...if they have a contract. They know if the other side doesn't live up to their end of the contract, the courts will make things right. Perhaps I'm paying you, who live on the other side of the world, millions of dollars for millions of widgets, and you don't come through with them. If I have no recourse in your country's legal system, or if our contract can't be honored by my country's legal system, you better believe I'm not going to do business with you—or in your country—ever again.

Apply this to marriage. Couples in a contract-based society believe that if they get married, the legal system will protect them during and after their marriage. We stake our fortunes and hopes on it. But where's the contract? It's either state marital law or it's your prenup. In either case, the courts question them only as little as humanly possible to preserve the country's legal glue.

BLAME THE BRITS

Now that you're contract-society initiated, settle in for a little time travel. First stop, ancient Greece, where the Greeks called love a sickness and said it was its own type of insanity. As the Romans conquered Greece, they deemed love acceptable, but only in extramarital dalliances. Marriages, these ancients believed, were sheerly practical unions. As their armies took over Europe, England, and beyond, their beliefs spread westward.

By the Middle Ages, settlements in England were following a loose set of laws, laws that occurred often enough to be considered legally de facto. These collectively came to be known as "common law." In the 1760s, one Sir William Blackstone collected and published these in a series titled *Commentaries on the Laws of England*. The term English Common Law (ECL) became part of the country's legal lexicon. Besides being a useful reference in England proper, Blackstone's tomes could be shipped off to English colonies, like those in America. Why does any of this matter? When I share some of America's crazier marital laws you'll see direct hand-me-downs from ye olden times. And you're about to agree to these laws via your marriage license.

English Common Law had some real gems when it came to

marriage. One edict from the 1500s stated, "The husband cannot be guilty of a rape committed by himself upon his lawful wife, for, by their mutual matrimonial consent and contract, the wife hath given herself up in this kind unto her husband, which she cannot retract." Translated, this nugget means there's no such thing as rape in a legal marriage. (Wonder how long it took to get that one totally off the books in every state? If you're thirty years old or more, it was during your lifetime. See the details in the Appendix timelines.)

Another cringer goes back to the start of this chapter when I mentioned women being viewed as property. America first declared independence from Britain in 1776. In 1765, Blackstone stated, "The very being and legal existence of the woman is suspended during the marriage, or at least is incorporated into that of her husband under whose wing and protection she performs everything." Translated, that means a woman ceases to exist as a separate, legally recognized entity when she gets married. In other words, after they exchanged vows of marriage, a husband and wife were legally one...just not "one" in the romantic sense that we think of today.

DOESN'T LOVE HAVE *ANYTHING* TO DO WITH MARRIAGE?

Ahh, romance... Prior to the mid- to late-1700s, not only was romantic love *not* a prerequisite for marriage, it was believed that no sensible person would actually select a life partner based on the fleeting nature of such emotions. Romantic love, everyone admitted, comes and goes. And it wasn't just the Greeks and Romans who thought as much.

In AD 1184 a French priest named Andreas Scapellanus wrote about the differences between the love and affections that exist between married men and women. "Love," he wrote, "can have no place between husband and wife, even if some couples do experience moderate affection." Yes, he conceded, romantic love did exist, but the place for its heady passion was between a husband and his mistress or a wife and her lover.

Later, French Renaissance philosopher Michel de la Montaigne also shared his skepticism about love and marriage. In AD 1580, de la Montaigne, who, incidentally, was married for decades, wrote, "If there is such a thing as a good marriage, it resembles friendship rather than love." Some argue that Shakespeare's *Romeo and Juliet*, which premiered in 1597, is a cautionary tale about the insanity of young romance. Seen thusly, it could be deduced that such madness has no place in the world of Montagues and Capulets.

In some cultures, these old beliefs continue to be best–practice beliefs. According to a backgrounder that the tour group China Educational puts out for its clients, "It is ok for adolescents to have feelings of love, but when they reach marriageable age then love is thought to be not only unnecessary but probably even dangerous. More useful and important to prepare for choosing a spouse would be a good education, having a job, and maybe owning a flat."

So how did modern Americans get so Cupid-headed about marriage? In the 1700s and into the early 1800s, revolutions in America and France were fueled by a citizenry who questioned everything espoused by prior establishments. Enlightenment thinkers of the era promoted the idea that people (well, white men at least) had a right to personal happiness. Prior to that, happiness didn't factor into the cultural fabric that made up Western society, and it certainly wasn't considered a right.

When the Declaration of Independence proclaimed, "We hold these truths to be self-evident, that all men are created equal, that they are endowed by their Creator with certain unalienable Rights, that among these are Life, Liberty and the pursuit of Happiness," that last word—happiness—set off an intense ripple effect.

In no time, the term "love match" became popularized, and "happily ever after" soon followed on its heels. Jane Austen wrote her romance-laden *Sense and Sensibility* in 1795, and for years, she turned out many more of the same. Austen was in good company—other Romantic Period writers included lover-poets like frothy Lord Byron.

By the mid-twentieth century, romance novels targeted teenage girls and the so-called feminine mystique was in full force in American suburbs. In 1950, a scant 23 percent of college undergraduates were women, a drop from the decade prior when they had either donned Rosie the Riveter coveralls or headed to campus while men were fighting in World War II. During the 1960s, the Pill was legalized nationwide (for married women at least), and Masters and Johnson outed the mechanics of sex when they published *Human Sexual Response*. By the end of that decade, US involvement in the Vietnam War had exploded, and, this time when men went off to fight, women headed back to campus, where they have remained ever since. When veteran men came home this time around, they returned to coeds on campus, a women's lib movement, *Roe v. Wade*, the Equal Rights Amendment, the Pill for all, and "irreconcilable differences" as a catch-all grounds for divorce.

All told, the puzzle pieces that informed the societal landscape of 2000–2020 were in place: women were earning advanced degrees, birth control was commonplace, and marriage was viewed as the unification of two loving partners who chose one another. American women were better positioned than ever to chart their own future. What could go wrong?

CHAPTER TWO

The Dreaded D-Word

MOST AMERICANS QUOTE THE ODDS OF A MARRIAGE LAST-
ing "Till death us do part" as fifty-fifty. (As of this writing, the
divorce rate is actually more like 44 percent, but I'm splitting
hairs.) While I'm no sociologist, I have sat through fifteen years
of divorce cases and worked with hundreds upon hundreds of
divorcing clients, all of which has afforded me an inside look
into the most private corners of fractured marriages. From that
vantage, it's obvious that what so many say rings true: the most
common thing that most couples argue about is money...but
leave it at that and you shortchange yourself, big-time.

Money goes hand in hand with so much that's vital to us as
individuals. The obvious two are power and control, but finances
also shape a person's identity, self-worth, aspirations, dreams,
freedom, joy, voice, generosity, pride, security, respect, health,
well-being, commitment...I could go on and on.

Of course, money isn't the answer to success in each of those
arenas. **But how two people in a couple interact financially
with one another touches on nearly every aspect of who each
is as an individual.** Like a tree with healthy roots that give way

to a solid trunk and protective canopy, a healthy financial inter-relationship between spouses creates a safe space for its partners to grow together, families to form, and loving bonds to flourish. And like a tree with unhealthy roots, a marriage based on an unhealthy financial relationship eventually topples over.

The old rules of how people interact in marriages with respect to all things financial no longer fit. Maybe, like me, you watched your parents manage money, just like they once watched their own parents. With these examples and relationships as references, we inadvertently soak up many of the same habits, roles, and perceptions. Subconsciously or not, what we witness as we grow up worms its way into our lives. It's like those insurance commercials in which thirty-somethings morph into their moms and dads, one elderly habit at a time. At some point, everyone will have the same "I'm turning into my parents!" epiphany.

Turning into our parents poses a problem because the financial constructs that worked (or didn't work) for them don't stand a chance of working for relationships today. The way we manage our finances and our households has not caught up to our financial realities. By the time most millennials (and Gen Zers, I predict) get married, they're in their thirties. Most have graduated from college and have been working for a while. They have managed their own budgets—well or poorly—and have accumulated some amount of assets and debts, as well as personal beliefs and habits around money.

My divorce clients fit this profile. They are, like you, smart, capable, professional people with degrees. They are evolved; I've never encountered one who believed women should putter around barefoot and pregnant in the kitchen. **They simply don't live the gender-stereotypical lives of the last century in any** arena—that is, except in the way they and their spouses have interacted financially.

The dichotomy is most glaringly obvious when I first meet with a female client in a heteronormative couple. After getting a grasp of her general story, I'll ask about her and her husband's marital estate. ("Marital estate" refers to the assets, liabilities, and property to be divided in a divorce.) I can't tell you how many times these women have no idea. Nearly to a person, they'll reply, "Well, he just said that he took care of it…" Then they'll share that their husband didn't offer up any information, and they didn't ask. Usually, they get embarrassed and admit that they thought they were supposed to trust him to manage their finances. lol no.

People in all couples and in all roles come by the willingness to sit in the dark honestly. After all, earlier generations of parents never spoke openly (and constructively) about money—among each other or with us. Do you know what your parents made in an average year? I don't. My parents came of age in the 1950s and started from the ground floor when they got married in the 1960s. Not only did we not talk about money, but as soon as I was out on my own, my "modern" financial picture was as foreign to them as theirs was to mine.

Given that, and given schools don't teach financial literacy, most couples today are left to sort money matters out on their own. As a result, countless couples cross their fingers and soldier on as one partner takes the reins and the other sticks their head in the sand. Both check their common sense at the marriage door and put their faith in the scripted happy endings advertised everywhere. What happens? If they follow outdated gender roles, and if they don't tackle financial matters with substantive conversations, they set themselves up for contention.

THE MYTH OF "MY" MONEY

Many clients come to our office thinking they are in for a simple division of assets, even though they never got a prenup. "We kept everything separate," these clients report. "The house is in my name, we kept separate bank accounts—what's theirs and mine is easy to see." I have to break the news to these souls that, because there is no prenup that states otherwise, regardless of its title, regardless of who paid what from which account, the appreciation and equity in that house that occurred after they were married are considered part of their marital estate. As such, the house does not wholly belong to either person; its gains belong to both of them, equally.

That's because once someone is hitched, in the eyes of the law there is no such thing as "my money," at least not outside the wedding-eve value of a premarital asset. (A premarital asset is something a spouse owned individually before the marriage.) From then on—at least, without a prenup that states otherwise—there is only "our money." After they marry, if one spouse opts to binge-watch Netflix on the couch rather than hold down a job, under the law, half of every paycheck their worker bee other half earns is considered rightfully theirs.

Here and there, minor insecurities and budding resentments around money crop up. The couple might address these as one-offs, slapping quick-fix Band-Aids on any wounded emotions. But as such, they don't confront the deep-rooted issue or issues that grew into resentment. And so they miss their chance to create far-reaching, fundamental financial solutions. When this gets repeated over and over, bandages fail to staunch the flow of hurt. Wounds never fully heal. Walls go up.

Now *that* conjures an unpleasant image. But that's not

where you're heading! By reading this book, you're already in the 10 percent of engaged couples who recognize the status quo won't work for you. And that bodes really well for your marriage. If you're already convinced your marriage will need more than crossed fingers, and you're ready to talk about something more consequential than wedding flowers, feel free to skip to the next chapter.

However, if you think you don't need to hash out anything with your partner beyond those flowers or the menu, I have some advice. If you're dying for a "big day," go for it. But just throw a really fantastic party—do not actually trade vows and stage a wedding ceremony. The stakes are too high. If you're on the fence, and doubt a divorce, let alone a messy one, can happen to you ("We talk about *everything...*"), keep reading.

DIVORCE SUCKS, EVEN FOR NICE PEOPLE

Most people who come into my office for divorce do not want to leave their spouse penniless and destitute. And nobody has ever come into my office and said, "Oooh! I want a long, expensive divorce case, please." Most people I represent just want their case over with as quickly, as painlessly, as fairly, and as inexpensively as possible. They only want their fair share, their children to be protected and cared for, and the entire matter sorted out and over with as soon as possible. Those are achievable goals, and I do everything to make each pan out.

Other folks—the vindictive ones and their close cousins, the ones seeking vindication—have different priorities. A vindictive client has one goal: cause their soon-to-be ex short- and long-term pain and/or discomfort. I weed these vengeful kinds out, because—aside from my moral obligations and belief in karma— if inflicting misery is someone's goal, they will *never* be happy.

Not with a case outcome, not with anything related to their ex, not with my representation, and on. There's never a real finish line for someone bent on that particular brand of revenge.

The ones hoping for vindication similarly are always disappointed. Typically, they have appointed themselves the virtuous spouse. They see a trial as the means to publicly establish themselves as the lily-white innocent and their partner as the rotten-to-the-core bad guy. They contest their divorce all the way to the courthouse for their moment on the stand. When called upon, they explain to the courtroom precisely the ways in which their other half acted the scoundrel. They dream the judge will then stand up and shout, "I'm horrified!" and then turn to the offending spouse to say, "Sir/Ma'am, it's all your fault! What a horrible excuse for a partner and/or parent you have been! I cannot believe you did this and this and this... *Clearly, no one* could be married to you. You are THE BAD GUY!"

But, because no one 100 percent ever wins in divorce, any satisfaction is short-lived. If a dressing down happens (odds are it won't), that's always followed by the job at hand. "Okay," the judge says next. "Now let's get to why we're all really here: here's the custody arrangement and the visitation schedule. Here's how you will divide the marital estate. Here's the schedule for alimony and child support. Case closed."

It goes like this because a judge's job is very specific: to divide a marital estate, set support (for a spouse and/or children), and make a custody schedule. If a "speech" happens, it's extra. It's not the point.

WHAT'S A "BAD" DIVORCE?

From my vantage as a lawyer, I consider some divorces to be good ones (uncontested, amicable relations, easily agreed upon settlement terms) and others to be bad ones. To qualify as a bad divorce, the bar is pretty low. First, a bad one is any divorce that can't be settled without going to arbitration or a trial. These are automatically expensive cases—here in Atlanta, where I practice, it is not unusual for each party to shell out $15,000 in legal fees for even short trials. Depending on what's at stake, the price goes up, possibly way up, from there. Next, a bad divorce is one that drags out. Inevitably, the longer the process takes, the more it costs. The divorce cases I've been trying in recent years have been averaging eighteen months (counting from when the initial request for a divorce is filed with the clerk of court). I've also seen it take years for a couple to reach even the barest of baseline agreements to finetune in mediation. My third and final qualifier—you had to see this coming—is any divorce without a prenup is a bad one. Not having a prenup inevitably adds time, expense, misery, and headaches to your proceedings.

HOW DIVORCE—ESPECIALLY A BAD ONE—SUCKS
Reason One: It Sucks Because the
Discovery Process Is a Major Pain

In a divorce, the "discovery process" involves each side exchanging financial and personal information with the other. Spouses fill out individual financial affidavits (sometimes called financial declarations, financial disclosures, or financial schedules), which list each person's monthly budget, assets, and debts. If one party challenges the other's affidavit, their lawyer will request documentation that verifies its information. In such a situation, it's very typical to ask for three to five years of a person's tax returns, W-2s, 1099s, pay stubs, bank account records, credit card statements, person-to-person payment systems (PayPal, Venmo, Bitcoin, Coinbase, etc.), retirement and investment account statements, and more.

On the personal side of this discovery step, it's not uncommon to drill deep into someone's social life, including their life on social media. For instance, one spouse's lawyer might ask the other spouse to log into their Facebook profile, download it, save it on a drive, and hand it over. That drive should include that person's public and non-public information on Facebook, including anything posted on their page, anything they've been tagged in, anything they have reacted to or commented on, and so on. The same chain of events could be applied to other social media accounts, email accounts, and the like.

Other types of "discoveries" include interrogatories (written questions that must be answered under oath), depositions (sworn and transcribed oral interviews between a lawyer and witnesses, defendants, and others), and more. Depositions alone can go on for hours on end, with every tick of the clock signifying a billable moment. Why does every kind of discovery suck, separately and collectively? This step devours time and money, and it is a hassle factory in overdrive thanks to all the wrangling it brings.

Reason Two: It Sucks Because the Other Side Can Drag Out a Case as They Wish

It's easy to intentionally delay a case, but there's very little that you can do to speed one up. When one party is faced with another that has dug in their feet, their only option is to give the other side exactly what they want. This might be worthwhile regarding assets or alimony, but what if children were at stake? Most parents don't fork over custody and rights when they believe that's not in the best interest of the kids. In that case, a person can choose to throw in the towel or pay still more legal fees and hope for the best outcome. What a crappy set of choices. And what a crappy place to be in.

DIVORCE AS FINANCIAL BLACKMAIL

I just finished a divorce case in which each party spent more than $125,000 in litigation fees—a quarter of a million dollars altogether. Their marital estate neither necessitated nor supported such costs. They had one mortgaged house, one mortgaged commercial rental space, and fifteen years of relatively minor savings, all of which were worth about a million dollars. They had one child, but couldn't agree on a visitation schedule.

The wife didn't want any part in fighting, but the husband vindictively filed motions left and right. And when either side files a motion, the other must respond, which means each party's billable hours keep mounting. The woman was stuck. As a strategy, this amounts to playing chicken with the terms of a divorce settlement—a particularly ruthless kind of financial blackmail. When this goes on long enough, a couple's marital estate dwindles, along with each person's portion of it.

Ultimately, between the guardian *ad litem* (a professional appointed by a judge to assess custody disputes), financial experts, attorneys, and on, this couple flushed away 25 percent of their entire net worth to reach a verdict.

Reason Three: It Sucks Because Some
Lawyers Just Want Your Money

My business strategy is simple: if I do right by my clients, they will send me more clients. But that's not every lawyer's approach. Many strategize to maximize billable hours and measure a case by its financial value. Family law attorneys in particular can get away with this approach because it's extremely easy to convince a divorcing client that the opposing party is being unreasonable. Divorce lawyers meet people at their most raw, most vulnerable, most fearful, and sometimes most volatile point in life, and some take advantage of the timing. Because of how our judicial system is set up, when a person's counsel doesn't have their best interest at heart, draining their resources (as well as those of the opposing party) isn't difficult.

Reason Four: It Sucks Because You Don't Know
Invasive Till You Go Through a Bad Divorce

In most types of litigation, a person's private life is irrelevant to the case. Not so in divorce cases. Take Georgia, for example. To get divorced in the Peach State, the couple must report the date their marriage separation began, which state law defines as the last time spouses had "marital relations." You read that correctly. What exactly qualifies as "marital relations?" That's part of the problem—relations may be a euphemism for sexual intercourse, but what qualifies as sexual? Or intercourse, for that matter? It's up to judges to define the details. Worse, still, it's the date a couple can *agree* they last had marital relations. If they disagree on the date, they will have to communicate to nail it down. Should they go through their lawyers to do so, they will be paying attorneys to argue over their sex life.

WHEN "SPECIAL PRIVILEGES" SABOTAGE A DIVORCE

I tend to try cases in metro Atlanta, where judges aren't necessarily sticklers about verifying marriage separation dates per state law (according to the last time a couple had intercourse). But there are some old-school judges in Georgia's rural counties who think differently. In one such case, the judge learned the divorcing pair had engaged in sex after their case had been filed, and he threw them out of his courtroom on the spot. He forced them to start their case over, beginning with a new petition for divorce. Consider that the next time you hear of a divorcing couple with "special privileges" or one that ends up in the bedroom together in an attempt to give their marriage another shot.

Reason Five: It Sucks Because No One Can Predict Anything about a Judge

Even the best attorney can't honestly say how a divorce case will go. When your case is filed with the clerk of court, it is randomly assigned to a family court judge in that county. That means an individual judge wields a lot of power over your future—even amidst division and settlement laws. And judges are regular humans with regular human biases and ideas.

I encountered one judge who would not sign off on a fifty-fifty, week-on, week-off split of physical custody and visitation, even though it was what both parents wanted. He said—in court, on more than one occasion—"I only saw my kids every other weekend and we had a great relationship. Week-on, week off doesn't work. It's not good for the kids."

Alimony can be a crapshoot, too. Some states have cookie-cutter guidelines to determine it. For instance, in Texas, if a divorcing couple had been married between ten to twenty years, one spouse would be entitled to five years of "maintenance awards" (a.k.a. alimony or spousal support). Should this pair have been married between twenty and thirty years, seven years of alimony is on the table. Texas law gets even more detailed and stipulates that support is not to exceed $5,000 a month or 20 percent of the paying spouse's average gross income—whichever is less.

However, most states don't have established, consistent alimony formulas. That means a person could be in one courtroom with a judge who says a spouse is deserving of five years of alimony at $2,000 a month. In the next courtroom over, a different judge could review exactly the same case, abide by exactly the same laws, and determine the spouse isn't deserving of alimony at all.

Reason Six: It Sucks Because Divorce Settlements and Proceedings Are Public Record

In most states, a divorce case (all its related documentation—prenup, separation agreement, depositions, financial affidavits, settlement, custody determinations, trial transcripts, etc.) is filed with the judicial system and becomes public record. Anyone can access matters of public record unless a judge has sealed a case, but even so, the court can be petitioned to release all or some of the files. When divorce records *are* sealed, it's usually to protect a minor. For example, a case involving a teen with an addiction might be kept private.

Reason Seven: It Sucks Because Airing Dirty Laundry Is Systematically Encouraged

I once objected over the relevancy of an opposing party's monologue about dirty laundry. Specifically, they took issue with the process my client had employed in order to remove sweat stains from their golf shirts. The whiner was slinging any kind of mud they could (lame, all of it) in an attempt to tip the scales of property division in their favor. It could have worked; dirty laundry and mudslinging can actually impact property division, and that possibility makes to sling or not a "can't hurt, might help" strategy for some. The gamble causes desperate types to throw as much dirt as possible just to see if any of it sticks. Any impact is, at best, slight, given judges usually lean in favor of a 50/50 split, or a 45/55 imbalance at most. Still, I've seen people spend hundreds of thousands of dollars for the slight advantage.

That day the judge answered my objection with, "I know, I know. But I've got to let them talk about it." They then turned to the garrulous grouch. "I'm telling you here and now I don't find anything about who washed whatever shirts in whatever way to be worthy of swaying my opinion one direction or the other," the judge said. "Still," they took a deep breath and exhaled, "you're permitted to put up your case, so I guess I have to let you continue."

CHAPTER THREE

A Crash Course in Prenups

THE CLIENT WHO SAT IN FRONT OF ME WAS AT THE TAIL end of a forty-three-year marriage. She told me the final straw for her was when her husband got caught forging her name on a loan. His desperate act didn't come out of nowhere, though. In their later years, she said he became stingy with money and would criticize her spending habits. Eventually, the criticism descended into flat-out verbal abuse.

She didn't exactly know what started the trouble. He was a numbers whiz with a lifelong career in the financial industry. He had always worked with money, and he was good with it. They had a huge house that sat on a ton of land, acreage they had planned to pass down to their children. She told me she had looked forward to leaving them better off than she'd ever had it. By the time I met her, their six kids were grown and they had put them all through college. She had occasionally worked as a seamstress, but, for the most part, was a homemaker. When I met her, she was sixty-two years old.

After she told me the bones of her story, we started looking at what her divorce would entail. I began by crossing child custody and child support off the list—the kids were adults, so those categories weren't relevant. Then I told her it looked like dividing assets and debts and sorting out alimony were really the only things on the table. So, I asked her, what are your assets?

"Besides the house and the land, I really have no idea," she answered. "You know, I...I believe we've got retirement. I believe he's got money saved up?" There were only two things she was sure of: he worked with Morgan Stanley on some investments—she had seen the name on those statement envelopes in the mailbox—and he'd been day trading some from his office in the guest house since he retired. As she saw it, he simply continued to do what he had done all those years that had earned them the big house and valuable land. They never had conversations with specifics about money and never talked about the state of their finances, household budget, or investments. Mailed statements and a hunch were pretty much the extent of her insight into their marital estate.

I thanked her, she left, and my team and I got to work digging into their finances. When we subpoenaed the bank and went through the records, we found her husband's chief stressor. The savings and the retirement money he had once apparently saved up—well over three million dollars—were nearly nonexistent. Turns out he'd gambled it away on the same stock for years. All that was left was $10,000. Before debts.

To tell you the truth, as I write this, I feel for the guy. For some reason, he had decided one particular stock was his ticket to an extra-comfy retirement. The one he'd become obsessed with might be eleven cents a share one day, then down to three cents the next, then back up to eight cents, and so on. When it was in the eleven-cent range, he raked it in. But, just like a lot of other investors, when it tanked, his investment withered. So he would jump out just before he lost absolutely everything, then watch the stock price closely.

I'm guessing, given how secretive he was and the enormous sum he lost, he stared at market tickers as attentively—and as obsessively—as a gambling addict watches the spinning dials of their lucky slot machine. Like a $5-a-spin slot machine, "penny stocks" (so-called because they are worth, you guessed it, mere pennies) probably seemed innocuous...at first. When the value would begin to rise anew, he'd invest again and the net value of his shares would pile up. I bet, like the casino-lover in the moments after they hit the jackpot, he was so awash in relief that he could finally exhale, deeply and fully. After all, he was raised in a time when men were expected to provide and to do so stoically.

But we know how it ended for this guy. The market dipped again, and he hopped back off the ride, and the cycle went round and round, year after year until he decimated the seven-figure stash that could have more than comfortably sustained him and his wife through their golden years. He whittled away at a nest egg that might have left their kids with a surplus, rather than the debts they now face. Going through all of that alone, shouldering all of that responsibility, and weathering all of that drama solo—self-imposed or not—had to have been hell.

As for my client, the wife, by the time we uncovered every-thing, her only recourse was to let the courts divvy up what was left—the land and the house. (Grant you, that's more than some retired divorcing couples have to start with.) Because they had married as teens and spent more than four decades together, she would have been a prime candidate for a lifetime of alimony, but you can't squeeze water from a rock. In cases such as hers, a judge can't do much, if anything. Debtor's prisons are a thing of the past, and what good would it do to jail an older man in his situation? Today, my former client is divorced and lives with one of their children. The rest of the kids pitch in to support her; the $300 her ex sends each month doesn't cover much. Some of them don't speak to their father.

Of all the questions we could ask about this case, what I think we should be asking is this: if this couple had established full transparency at the start of their marriage, would he have played the stock market with their retirement account? If he was legally obligated to share his strategy and actual dollar-amount figures, year in and out, would things have gotten so bad? Would she have gone along with his approach? Were his financial anxieties inevitably going to lead to abuse? Or, by being transparent and honest about money, by setting up a relationship that was a true partnership, would their marriage, their family home, and their children's inheritance be saved?

My client's scenario is not something that happens in a marriage guided by and built on transparency. It also doesn't happen when your prenup sets ground rules that direct how you and your spouse will interact over money.

REALITY CHECK

Engaged couples today are like a pair of well-established corporations on the precipice of a massive financial merger. It would be insane to merge two financial entities such as these without an agreement created by legal professionals. Anyone would need, in writing, how the two agreed to join and operate these "companies," right? Right.

If you've made it through the preceding chapters (and perhaps also reviewed the timeline of psycho-marriage and divorce laws in the Appendix), and you're still considering marriage, you might be feeling a bit…uneasy. After years of divorce cases, I understand. Having personally been in your shoes, I get it, acutely. But the answer is not a broken engagement, swearing off marriage, or playing ostrich. Solutions exist, but they are grounded in something most people in the thick of wedding planning are not terribly interested in—a major reality check. This brings me to the five cold, hard truths anyone entering marriage must face.

One: Life is unpredictable. People change and situations change.

Two: The person whom you love most in the world today can end up being someone you barely know tomorrow. (You signed up for thirty-something Frank, but the fifty-something Frank? The guy in the thick of his midlife crisis who just spent your family savings on a luxury yacht? No, you've absolutely never met him. Who would head to the altar with *that* Frank?)

Three: Given points one and two, there is no guarantee that any marriage is forever.

Four: You absolutely, positively do not want to be in a bad divorce.

Five: A bad divorce counts as one that racks up time and money (all of them), hits you in the gut at the worst time (all of them), makes public how you split assets and debts (all of them), determines custody (all of them, for those who have children), and/or plays out in a public courtroom (some of them, though there's no predicting which ones).

Okay. There. You did it, you looked reality in the face and weathered it. Nice job. Now let's look at what prenups are—and aren't. Then we'll take a top-level tour of the steps you'll take in Part Two, where the working chapters of the book are housed.

WHAT EXACTLY IS A PRENUP?

A prenup is a set of rules that dictates how your finances are to be handled after marriage—and if powered up, prescription-style, during it as well. It legally supersedes the marital laws in the state with jurisdiction over the divorce. The document is written in legalese and formatted according to legal standards. Prenups are commissioned by one or both parties, and, when everything therein is mutually agreed upon, each person indicates their consent via signature. The signed document is then either tucked away somewhere in the couple's house (hopefully in a fireproof, locked safe) or in a bank's safe-deposit box.

If a divorce is later sought by a couple with a prenup, the divorce lawyer for the petitioner (the person initially seeking the divorce) will draft a divorce settlement agreement based on terms in their premarital agreement. When the settlement agreement is mutually approved and signed, it is filed. This document works its way through the county court system and gets assigned to a randomly selected judge.

From there, the path might change, depending on the case's governing state. In South Carolina, for example, that judge reviews the settlement document (and other filed material as is relevant). Should there be no hiccups, both spouses and their respective representatives next appear before the judge and the latter then approves their request for divorce and settlement terms. After the judge initials the couple's settlement agreement, the magistrate drafts and signs a divorce decree (an official court order that declares the marriage dissolved). From there, the decree and the case's supporting paperwork are filed with the local clerk of the court's office. By filing the papers as such, the case becomes accessible to one and all as its documentation is then considered public record. And so it is that a couple's marriage union is legally dissolved.

That's the bare-boned, basic path a divorce takes when a couple has a classic prenup. But a prescribed prenup goes further than the classic model. To get a prescribed prenup, a couple works three specific steps that yield a blueprint for their daily financial interactions, a blueprint that radically affects their marital relationship.

PRESCRIBED STEP ONE: LAY BARE YOUR CURRENT FINANCES

The first step of *The Prenup Prescription* addresses what a person brings to the marriage. It covers your premarital assets and debts, which, in addition to sketching how each affianced person looks financially, also illuminates their personal habits around money. To get this snapshot on paper (and to make the prenup legally enforceable), each party fills out, then exchanges, personal financial affidavits. (This is an itemized list of an individual's debts and assets.) This step, which is fully addressed in Chapter Four, embodies the core marriage tool of transparency.

PRESCRIBED STEP TWO: SET UP YOUR ACCOUNTS AND SORT YOUR FINANCES

This step marks the biggest point of difference between a prescribed prenup and those that are run-of-the-mill. In step two, a couple spells out how they will set up their finances—from bank accounts to bill paying—and how they will share that information with one another. It likely includes spending safeguards, too. Step one is about what you will merge; step two is how you will merge what you both have. It exercises the core marriage tool of communication.

PRESCRIBED STEP THREE: PLAN FOR THE FUTURE

The third step addresses contingency plans—set plans that may be needed should certain events occur. While most people think of divorce settlement agreements (the legal document detailing the division of a marital estate and spousal support terms) as the one and only contingency plan in a prenup, there are many others to consider.

For instance, you can address other plans like

- wills;
- life insurance;
- medical insurance;
- retirement savings, etc.

While the particulars of these "extras" *can't* be folded into a prenup, each party's commitment to create, maintain, and share them *can* be included at a top level. For example, you might have a clause that states something like, "Jan will establish and maintain her own life insurance policy, and will share access and updates on this policy with Lexi on an annual basis." Including these types of clauses is a prime example of how a prenup can dictate behavior, and thus, make adherence to it a legal obligation. Step three also can include trigger clauses that both spouses must follow before they can file for divorce (like attending therapy together). While contingency planning tends to stir up doomsday fears, it also has a silver lining: it requires each party to commit to the core healthy marriage tool of fairness.

Now that you know what prenups are, let's dive into what they aren't.

DON'T BELIEVE EVERYTHING YOU HEAR

After fifteen years of speaking engagements, podcast appearances, networking events, and everyday socializing, I have heard countless prenup myths and misconceptions. As a self-appointed prenup evangelist, I am obligated to shut down that disinformation cycle. Let's tackle some of the most common things I encounter with a short session of True or False.

True or False: People who get a prenup expect they will divorce their partner.

False: Prenups are divorce insurance.

If I had a dollar for every time I heard this one...I've been asked *ad infinitum* if getting a prenup is the same as admitting defeat in a marriage before you've said, "I do." Number one, there is no statistic that supports this—I have yet to see a study that shows people who signed prenups are more likely to get divorced than couples who do not sign prenups. And number two, every person I've met who wants a prenup plans on staying married.

I think this falsehood is a knee-jerk reaction to what's essentially insurance against a bad divorce, and it doesn't bear out. With a prenup, you ensure that *if* you get divorced, it won't be as complicated, time-consuming, and expensive as if you didn't have your "policy." Apply that line of thinking to the idea of car insurance. Does everyone with car insurance believe they're going to have a catastrophic accident? I sure hope not. But, by paying the premiums, they acknowledge the reality that such an accident is possible. They are insuring against the *possibility* that they might get in a catastrophic accident. Planning for the possibility of something does not mean you are planning to make that thing happen.

Moreover, having car insurance doesn't mean a driver suddenly doesn't worry about having an accident and drives recklessly. Most insured drivers do everything in their power to prevent having an accident and rely on their insurance safety net. The same goes for life insurance. Even if you have life insurance, you're still going to do everything in your power to not die.

And so it is for couples who get prenups. Just like any other couple, they are going to do everything in their power to make their marriage work. Calling on the insurance policy powers of a prenup is always a last resort.

True or False: Prenups aren't legally enforceable and can be overturned easily.

False: A solid prenuptial agreement is enforceable 99.9 percent of the time.

According to Google, "Are prenups enforceable?" is the most common question people have about the documents. So let me clear this one up. If you are in the 0.1 percent of people whose prenup is thrown out, it means one (or more) of three things.

Reason One: There was an omission or misrepresentation of material facts at the time that both parties signed the prenup. This goes back to contract law and America's reliance on it. To opt out of one marriage contract (state laws dictating all things marital finances) and opt into your own marriage contract (your prenup), you must know precisely what you're giving up. For instance, when one half of a couple doesn't divulge they own a plane in their financial affidavit, there's no way for the other half of the couple to know that if they hadn't signed that prenup with its clause about premarital assets, they would own a portion of that plane. The weird part is that you don't have to know the state laws you're signing up for when you get married, but you do have to know them if you want to opt out via a prenup.

This isn't just lousy red tape, if you think about it. Being full-on honest in a prenup's requisite financial affidavit can be critical to a marriage in myriad ways. For example, someone would make different decisions about how to manage money—before, during, and possibly after—a marriage if their spouse is worth negative $1 million versus positive $1 million. Bottom line: if you hide your debts or assets or income from your spouse, your prenup could be thrown out.

Reason Two: A prenup might get thrown out if one party signed under duress. If someone holds a gun to your head and says, "Sign this document," you are considered to have been under duress. Anything you sign in such a situation is unenforceable. This is pretty straightforward, but if you want to hear about one such case I tried (minus the gun), see the cautionary tales in the Appendix.

Reason Three: A prenup can be thrown out if a judge rules it was "unconscionable." That means that when the agreement was made, one party was significantly and unjustly favored, and that party secretly intended it to be as such. In the state where I practice, there has never been a prenup that was thrown out for being unconscionable. In other words, the courts here have never agreed with a counsel's argument for a prenup to be thrown out due to it being unconscionable. (There's a real-life example of this, too, in the cautionary tales in the Appendix.)

True or False: Most couples who get prenups are sugar daddies with gold-digging sugar babies.

False: That scenario represents a tiny, tiny percentage of those who get prenups.

When I am in front of an audience, I'll ask them to describe what comes to mind when someone says "prenup." To a person, they'll describe a sugar daddy/sugar baby scenario wherein one party is younger and less (or un-) established, and the other is an older mogul, successful celebrity, or person from an extremely wealthy family. The assumption is that the marriage is driven in defense of the younger, less well-off baby's thirst for the daddy's money. In that setup, the prenup serves to protect one spouse from the other. Why does that storyline get more play? You tell me. Which makes better clickbait: "Billionaire Leaves Decades-Younger Wife Penniless after Divorce. Prenup Screwed Her Over!" or "Jan and Lexi Smith Split Assets Evenly and Avoid Divorce Court Thanks to Their Prenup!"? No, prenups are not just for *Page Sixers* and Hollywood types, it's just that those salacious cases garner the most attention.

True or False: Prenups are expensive. Only rich people need them and only rich people can afford them.

False: Prenups are a lot less expensive than a wedding or a divorce, and they are well within the reach of most professionals.

Most decent prenups run a few grand each. (I've seen some online for $599, but let's just say you get what you pay for.) As for prenups only being for rich folk? Chris Rock once did a bit in which he talked about just that. He said people think prenups are for rich people, but they've got it backward. Half of $20 million leaves $10 million, he said, so it's no big deal for millionaire couples to split things—living on $10 million is not a struggle. But, he said, if you make $30,000 and your ex is awarded half of that? Now *that's* when you feel it and *that's* the couple who wishes they had a prenup.

LET'S COMPARE COSTS

If a prenup's price tag gives you pause, consider your wedding budget. The average cost of a wedding in the early 2020s is just shy of $30,000. Brides buy gowns that cost more than a prenup. That's typically a gown you wear once, right? Just sayin'...

True or False: Prenups take tons of time to pull together.

False: All told, the entire process should take thirty days or less.

Between pulling together your financial affidavits, hashing out how you'll set up your finances, determining your contingencies, and then sharing all that with your lawyers, the prenup process adds up to about a thirty-day process at worst. The most time-consuming part for couples tends to be filling out each person's financial affidavit. For some people, that just entails downloading info from a budget-tracking app or online spreadsheet. For others, it can take a few hours, or even a few hours over a few days, to get organized. Regardless of the timeframe, it's a non-negotiable necessity for both people to undertake when they commit to marry. Not only do you need to gather and share the information to successfully manage your household, but you will also need an up-to-date affidavit any time you get a loan for a significant purchase, like a house.

If adding one more thing to your to-do list seems unbearable at this point (after all, you're likely trying to work, plan a wedding, etc.), consider the mountain of legal documents buying something like a house entails. Then consider the one-page application you filled out for your marriage license. One page? Don't you want to dedicate a little more effort (and paperwork) to the relationship that could divide that house? Haven't you spent more time at showers, registering, or your bachelor/bachelorette parties? Isn't securing your financial future and setting your marriage up for success worth at least that same amount of time?

True or False: A prenup only protects the client of the lawyer who drafted it.

False: ...As long as you get a good prenup lawyer who's aiming for fairness.

One night out with a bunch of other lawyers, I overheard a veteran family law attorney say, "Prenups only protect your client, not the other spouse." Statements like that drive me *nuts*. I hear a lot of family law attorneys giving bad advice, but this falsehood in particular really sets me off. I guess the ignorance probably stems from prenups being rare enough that even experienced family law attorneys may only do one every three years. Whatever. Let's break down the facts.

seperate lawyers (x) each person!

Any basic prenup should ease the dissolution of a marriage, and save both parties time, money, and hassle in a divorce. The prenups I prescribe do that, but they also include terms designed to bolster a couple's marriage through transparency, communication, and fairness. When a couple creates the blueprint of a prescribed prenup, they cement those three tools as cornerstone principles of their marriage. So no, prenups do not just benefit the party who hired the drafting lawyer. They serve the best interest of both spouses.

QUESTIONS, SO MANY QUESTIONS...

Debunking those prenup myths only goes so far as to answer the scores of questions thrown in the path of a premarital agreement evangelist such as myself. Here are a few common queries I field.

Question: Can I DIY our prenup?

Answer: No. The number one reason you should work with a legal professional is that you don't know what you don't know. The second reason is that there is extremely specific language that must be in your prenuptial agreement for it to be enforceable. Would you stake your entire financial world, every single dollar that is in your life at the time that you get divorced—on a document that you winged?

A prenup could be standing between you and at least $15,000 in legal costs, plus up to a year and a half in court. I suppose you *could* go DIY, much like you could do your own dental work. You might get lucky and not screw up your teeth, but it's less than advisable to give it a shot. Same for buying a house. You wouldn't close on your own house by yourself, would you? Prenups are complicated and nuanced. They are something that you absolutely need to get right. Save DIY for wedding planning, your flowers, or favors.

Question: Should we each get lawyers?

Answer: The general rule is yes because while one lawyer drafts the document to include two people, they can only give legal advice to the one person who hired them to do the work. But it isn't about being sneaky or manipulative. Each person deserves their own expert to review the agreement, because, though it is ideally a benevolent document, there are certain truths to consider. One is that the spouse who is going to be the breadwinner is going to have different concerns than the spouse who puts their career on pause to devote themselves to, say, raising children. Having your own lawyer means you have someone to interpret the legalities and their implications. They might pull you aside to say, "Here are some things you might want to think about. I want to make sure that you're not agreeing to something unwittingly before understanding the ramifications of how it applies to you."

Question: What happens if we don't live in the state where we got our marriage license or had our wedding?

Answer: Marriage laws move with you. Because I am based in Atlanta, there's a clause in every prenup I've ever drafted that says, "This agreement is being signed under the laws of Georgia and the parties agree that it will be interpreted under the laws of Georgia." That means even if you move to another state, because the agreement was legal when and where it was signed, other states must enforce it. That kind of clause is standard for prenups, so if it's not in yours, ask for it to be added.

Question: Do prenups include anything about child custody or child support?

Answer: No. Child custody and support are the two main categories that cannot be addressed in a prenup. There are basically four categories of decisions to be made in any divorce case. There's the division of assets and debts, alimony, custody, and child support. Prenups can address the first two—the division of assets and alimony—but not the last two. That's because custody has to do with what's in the best interest of the children, a decision that can only be made at the time of the divorce, as it's based on the abilities of the parents at that moment. When a prenup is written, it may be for two very capable human beings. But at the time the two same people get divorced, things could have drastically changed in a way that renders one or both of them unfit or incapable of caring for children. Someone could also be heavily involved in a child's life when that child is five, but be completely absent by the time they turn ten, or vice versa.

Question: Can we put our dogs in our prenup?

Answer: Yes. You can address pet custody in a prenup. (These have earned the nickname "pet-nups.") Courts have determined pets to be property, so because prenups address property division, couples can include pet ownership and conditions. That might show up since premarital pets go to one spouse in the case of divorce, or it could be future pets will belong to spouse one or belong to spouse two.

....

Part Two

....

CHAPTER FOUR

Step 1: Lay Bare Your Current Finances

Marriage Tool: Transparency

IT'S ALMOST COMICAL HOW TABOO FINANCIAL TALK IS IN our culture. It can be considered rude—gauche, even—to disclose your income or your debt. Because this taboo has been encoded in so many of us, no one starts dating with the full-on truth. I don't know about you, but I have never sat down for a first date and opened with, "Hi, I'm Aaron, and I've got $20,000 in credit card debt and $100,000 in student loans. Nice to meet you! Oh, and, now that I think about it, I haven't saved nearly as much for retirement as I would have hoped by now..."

I'm not saying people should come out with everything the first time they meet, but I hear over and over "There was no really convenient time to ask (or tell)..." Why is that confession so commonplace in the office of divorce lawyers? I blame our culture for grooming people to accept marriage proposals without having a clue what their "person" looks like when they are fiscally disrobed. And I blame it for keeping people ignorant with regard to the economic implications of marriage.

Finances are not going to be covered in your premarital counseling, your event planner certainly won't bring up the subject if they can help it, and your friends are focused on throwing wedding-related parties. By the time the invitations have gone out, parents have most likely thrown up their arms and accepted that the big-day train has left the station. And that's how it happens that most people—on either side of the ask—don't know what they are signing up for until far too late.

BRAVO!

It's time for a dap, fist bump, a high-five, an elbow, or whatever people are doing by the time you read this. Why? If you do nothing else other than this one step, you are already ahead of 80 to 90 percent of the divorce clients I see in my office. By baring your financial self to your partner, you've escaped the clutches of the majority—a crew who would rather dance their first dance across a field of angry fire ants over delving into personal money matters. Keep that in mind as you read this chapter, and remember it if either you or your partner gets anxious or embarrassed working this step.

As I type, I'm looking out the window at my cookie-cutter development. Just like in any other such community, some neighbors are up to their eyeballs in debt. And others are living far below their means. From here, I can't tell one from the other.

I'm not casting dispersions. Society today enables living a lie and even celebrates it. We move in Facebook/Instagram/fill-in-the-blank-with-the-platform-du-jour lives and only show people the highlight reel. And—be honest—at no time does anyone put up a façade more than when they want someone to stick around for a romantic relationship.

When I used to pick up a date in my beat-up Honda Civic, there was little to no chance of hiding that I wasn't rich. Even so, these women didn't know how much debt I had (a lot), and I certainly never shared my net worth. That's because no one divulges the truth of their personal finances when they're out to impress a potential mate. And so the lies get perpetuated. Once a couple gets as close as they could possibly get—physically naked (or sometimes even tougher, emotionally naked)—who wants to get fiscally naked, too? C'mon! A person can only take so much nakedness.

But what happens when your dream person discovers you've been wooing them for years with dates and gifts you could never afford? What do they think five years in when they find out that fancy first date dinner still haunts your credit card balance?

THE CREDIT CONSPIRACY

Speaking of credit cards, our country's overall financial illiteracy makes for big business. I'll never understand why schools teach trigonometry and calculus when only about 2 percent of students will use those after graduation. But personal economics, the subject that is going to be important to 100 percent of students, is offered only sparingly, and usually only as an elective. Outside of what used to be called Home Ec (now referred to as "Life Skills"), future generations don't learn to balance their accounts or create basic household budgets. That means they're not going to learn, except by experience, why you should pay off your credit cards every month. And credit card companies certainly aren't interested in letting anyone know. Why? If you don't carry a balance, they don't make money. The entire industry is built on the assumption people will be bad with money.

There's a particularly loaded credit trap engaged couples can fall into, one that centers on engagement rings. If the ring buyer in your twosome is like most Americans in their position today, they can't afford to buy a hefty rock outright. More than likely, they'll put some money down on it and (hopefully) pay the rest off monthly. And (also hopefully) they'll finish the payments before your honeymoon. Why? If they don't, the ring recipient will be on the hook for the outstanding balance right there alongside their sweetheart. Because, technically speaking, as I keep saying, after the ceremony, what's their debt is your debt, what's their asset is your asset, and on...

Let's spell it out in dollars and sense (pun intended), with you as the ring recipient. Say the ring costs $5,000 retail, and its buyer got a shiny new card just to pay for the thing. (They didn't mention the card to you, of course; after all, they intended to pay it off solo. And a gift is supposed to be a gift, right?) If the credit card company charged 18 percent for the loaned money, and the buyer only forked over the card's minimum payment each month, it could take decades to pay your ring off. Even worse, by the time the card was paid off, your love token's total out-of-pocket cost would be more along the lines of $80,000, thanks to that 18 percent.

Alternatively, let's say the buyer put the ring on one of their existing cards. After the wedding, each of you decides to pool your income. If you and your spouse use this joint account to pay off lingering balances and outstanding bills, among other things, you, the bling-wearer will be more or less paying for your ring. Imagine waking to that revelation years down the line, perhaps in the middle of an argument over credit cards.

I can't count the number of clients who have sought out

my services after one too many such awakenings. In the really crummy cases, the new truths keep coming. It's not uncommon for people to first learn that they're actually dead broke or even a millionaire only when they are going through a divorce. Either epiphany slaps into understanding they have lived a lie. One set has lived beyond their means and now faces dire consequences. The other set knows money can't buy back the years they spent worrying, skimping, and struggling.

In a marriage, when you're not transparent, when you don't make decisions together, and when you don't solve problems together, you forge a path straight to my office. But you can head in the opposite direction. Choose to act with transparency and put compassion before judgment and fear, and you stand the best chance of never meeting me or my kind.

WHAT'S A FINANCIAL AFFIDAVIT?

To render a prenup legal (in almost every state), each person must fill out a financial affidavit. Even if they are not required where you live, you'll need the information one contains to follow *The Prenup Prescription*. So grab your phone, tablet, laptop, etc., and search for your state's *divorce* affidavit (you read that correctly; see "The Best Form for the Job"). Call it up right now—right now—because I'm about to jump into the world's shortest Intro to Financial Affidavits tutorial. It's much easier to follow along when you have one in front of you. Got yours? Good.

A financial affidavit (also called a financial declaration, financial disclosure, or financial schedule) is a formal statement that lists a person's assets, debts, and income. An asset is something you own that has a positive value. A debt is money you owe a person, institution (i.e., a credit card company, mortgage lender, car dealership, university, etc.), or other entity. The remaining balance owed on any loan you are indebted to pay counts as a debt. Income is money that you acquire (it's "incoming"). Income can be in the form of wages, project fees, interest, child support, alimony, tax refunds, gifts, and so on. When you sign your personal financial affidavit, you legally commit to its accuracy. Tada! That's all you need to know. Consider financial affidavits demystified.

GET THE BEST FORM FOR THE JOB

To work *The Prenup Prescription*, download the financial affidavit of the state where you live now, the one it requires each spouse to fill out in the event of a divorce. Why? Divorce affidavits include monthly expenses, which are critical to merge finances as newlyweds. Plus, if you give a set of completed divorce affidavits to a family law attorney, they can cull what's needed to populate the prenup version. Just be sure to keep those lists of monthly expenses near at hand so you can work step two.

In my experience, gathering the information to fill out a personal financial affidavit tends to be the most time-consuming part of the entire prenup process for a client. When I task a couple with filling them out, one person usually looks at the other in a way that tells me who will be done with theirs in a flash and who's going to take...longer. If you fall into the second category, there's literally no time like the present. Not only is it good practice to be familiar with your current financial standing, but it's also something every adult needs to know. The good news is that the information isn't difficult to get your hands on.

Go online to find out what's in your bank accounts, check

what's in your retirement, and get a Kelley Blue Book estimate for the value of your car...any of these take about sixty seconds to look up. Use Zillow or other such sites for a ballpark estimate of what your home is worth.

To make it really easy on yourself, start using an app to sync and track your financial accounts, autopay bills, and personal budget in real time. (I like Mint, it's from the same people behind TurboTax.) If managing finances isn't your strong suit, or if you decide as a couple that an app will be the best way to keep each other abreast of money matters, let this chapter serve as your starting line.

Here are some more solid budgeting tools:

- YNAB ("You Need a Budget");
- Goodbudget;
- EveryDollar;
- Personal Capital;
- PocketGuard;
- Honeydue; and
- Fudget.

People often get confused about what to list as an asset or property. Stick with listing items that you have had appraised and/or insured. Beyond that, include any personal items—heirlooms, art and jewelry, antiques, collections, and sentimentals—you'd hate to lose in a breakup. For the record, most used sofas are not worth anything of note. Unless yours happens to be a museum-worthy antique that could be auctioned off at Christie's, don't list it as an asset.

- Bank accounts
- investment accounts
- 401 K/retirement
- car debt and/or value
- Business
- student loans
- other debt?

DO I HAVE TO DISCLOSE *EVERYTHING?*

If you aren't transparent on your financial affidavit—if you've stashed assets, hidden income streams, or covered up debts—it's not a factual document and when the truth comes out, your prenup will be useless in court.

For my part, I can control the accuracy and legal qualifications of your document, but I can't control either party's honesty. No lawyer can. No one can predict—or police—a person determined to be financially dishonest, even if they stray into being "only a little bit dishonest."

There are aspects of a marriage for which 100 percent transparency isn't a necessity, nor is it really helpful. If my wife doesn't tell me she hates the way my hair grows on the back of my neck, which renders her 98 percent honest because she held back 2 percent over that gripe? Not a problem. But when it comes to financial affidavits, only 100 percent honesty is acceptable. In fact, because I am powerless to ensure the accuracy of this data, I include a clause in my client contracts that states I am not accountable for either party's honesty. I run the clause in big, bold print to be utterly clear.

Every now and then a prospective client still doesn't get it. "Do I really have to list *all* my assets and debts?" this person typically pushes. There's only one answer to that: yes. Yes, you do have to share *all* of it. Legally speaking, you must. But there's also a bigger issue to address.

If you're at odds over full disclosure in principle, it's time to be honest with yourself and ask if this—marriage—is really the kind of relationship you want to be in. Marriage is certainly not for everyone. And trust me, no one wants to be tangled up in marital laws unless they and their would-be spouse are really sold on legally committing. My dad has always said that marriage requires a person to be "committed to the idea of commitment." If you're not all-in, if you're not ready for full transparency, either plan for a short marriage or don't get hitched in the first place.

If you're on the other side of the fence, and perhaps are a naturally paranoid and confession-prone person obsessing about the chance you forgot some college-era account that still has $20 in it, ease up. Twenty bucks isn't going to invalidate your agreement. But if you are found to have been hiding something significant (a house, big debt, a business), *that* would matter, and a court will cite your secret as grounds to invalidate your prenup.

Make-or-break honesty and transparency go back to contract law. The point of a financial affidavit is to let both parties know exactly what they are waiving rights to and responsibilities for in exchange for the terms of their prenuptial agreement. If assets or debts are not listed by one or both sides, one or both parties are not making an informed decision to waive the rights state marriage laws grant them.

If both parties turn in fraudulent financial affidavits, then the prenup is null and void altogether. If one has innocently signed a prenup with one valid affidavit (theirs) and a fraudulent affidavit (the other party's), then it's up to Mr./Mrs. Innocent to either enforce the prenup's terms or opt instead for state law. The guilty party has no say in the matter.

All that adds up to the technical answer. But seriously, don't go there with secret stashes. Not only is it wrong, but also it'll most likely ruin your marriage—and for good reason. If that doesn't motivate you, there's this thing called forensic accounting and it'll get you busted. Promise.

FISCAL NAKEDNESS = TRANSPARENCY = ESSENTIAL IN MARRIAGE

Being transparent about your finances—putting your assets, debts, income, and expenses down on paper and showing it to your future spouse—sets a tone for your marriage, establishes full disclosure as a principle, and shows your commitment to honesty. In the same way you recite vows that detail how you'll treat your spouse, filling out a financial affidavit declares your intent to be transparent and honest.

Setting an expectation of monetary transparency spills into other aspects of a relationship. When you give your spouse-to-be your financial affidavit, you've just put a deposit into your pending marriage's "trust" account. Along those lines, every time you do other transparent acts—even something as simple as leaving your phone-facing screen up and unlocked on the coffee table—you've made another deposit in that account. Phone transparency—perhaps going so far as to share your lock code—may seem insignificant. But when either partner hides little things, over time those tend to chip away at a marriage. Little pieces of trash, it's been said, are what leads to great big piles of trash.

There is no other better, nor more convenient time to establish transparency with your spouse than right now. Now, before you are married, is the time for you to tell your intended you have $100,000 in IRS debt. The same goes for them. These confessions might make for uncomfortable conversations, but anyone getting married needs to get used to awkward conversations.

Plus, the payoff is real. When you commit to acting transparently, it develops into a default behavior. Call it muscle memory, learned behavior, rewiring...whatever it is, when a couple completes and shares financial affidavits, they pave their way to an open, honest marriage. Conversely, by the time a client hires me for their divorce, the trust account they shared with their partner is inevitably overdrawn, and their marriage is outright bankrupt.

CHAPTER FIVE

Step Two: Set Up Your Accounts and Sort Your Finances

Marriage Tool: Communication

ONCE YOU'RE MARRIED, YOU DON'T OWN WHAT YOU THINK you own, and you do own what you didn't think you owned. (How's that for a tongue twister?) More simply put, the law views ownership of a married couple's assets and debts differently than how modern couples do.

In everyday life, people assign ownership to things in three ways: mine, yours, or ours. Our mindset is that these things are yours, these things are mine, and these things we share. That's your laptop. These are my clothes. Those are your earrings. This is my iPhone. This is our house. Those are our cars. That's how we talk in our day-to-day lives.

Right now I'm working on *my* computer, and over there is *my* phone. Of course these things belong to me, right? Wrong.

I'm married. And as a married person, if I were to refer to who owns what based on standard marital laws, I'd be saying this is our desk, our computer, our phone. The judicial system may have shifted away from the old rules—"everything belongs to the husband"—but it's not moved much. Now the laws reflect "everything is owned by the marriage itself." No matter how you set up your 401(k), no matter whether you've had your house for years before you met your spouse, no matter if you were the one to pay off your SUV—*status quo* marriage law in all fifty states lumps these things into one big pile. That's why you need a prescribed prenup and why Step Two is integral to making yours dynamic.

Follow this step to spell out precisely who owns what in your marriage and who is responsible for what, financially speaking. The system I evangelize revolves around three "buckets:" Mine, Yours, and Ours. These buckets organize your finances in a way that reflects and formalizes people's everyday ownership norms. And now, let's begin...

WELCOME TO THE WORLD OF THREE-BUCKET BUDGETS

Picture a trio of buckets labeled respectively with Mine, Ours, Yours. "Mine" represents the money we both agree is mine to spend. "Yours" represents the money we agree is yours to spend. "Ours" represents the money we pool together. To best follow The *Prenup Prescription*, you'll need to employ one of two bucket models. Each model represents how money flows from one bucket—Mine, Yours, Ours—into another.

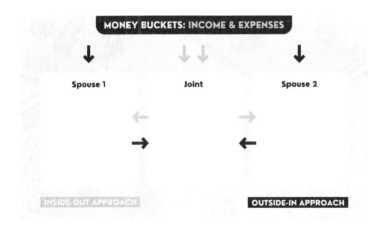

INSIDE-OUT BUCKET MODEL

In the Inside-Out Bucket Model, all money that comes to either of the spouses first flows into the Ours bucket to completely pool a couple's income. Next, two pre-set, agreed-upon portions are withdrawn from the Ours bucket and deposited into the Mine and Yours buckets. The money in each of these personal buckets is that person's to spend.

feels most natural (mc)

🗙 OUTSIDE-IN BUCKET MODEL

The second approach is the direct opposite of the Inside-Out Bucket Model. In the Outside-In Bucket Model, all money that comes to either spouse first flows into their personal Mine bucket. Next, a pre-set, agreed-upon portion from each of their personal buckets is withdrawn and deposited into the Ours bucket, thus, pooling their individual incomes.

Bills, College fund for kids,

Here's how the Outside-In Bucket structure would play out with actual dollar amounts if each spouse applied a one-third contribution. When this couple's paychecks are direct deposited into their own separate accounts (a.k.a. their personal buckets), they each put one-third of their total paycheck into their shared "Ours" bucket.

	MINE	OURS	YOURS
Individual Gross Annual Incomes	$100,000	∅	$50,000
One-Third Portion of Individual Gross Annual Income	$33,333	∅	$16,667
Personal Bucket Balances After Contributions	$66,667	$33,333 + $16,667	$33,333
Gross Annual Bucket Balances	$66,667	$50,000	$33,333

This approach represents a fair-share Outside-In model wherein each spouse deposits a pre-set agreed-upon portion of their individual incomes (one-third) into their joint account (their Ours bucket). The funds in the Ours bucket will go toward agreed upon-shared expenses. To opt for this model, a couple skims an equal percentage off of each person's personal income and deposits those amounts into the Ours bucket.

For contrast, consider if you were to split the cost of a household bill fifty-fifty (like roommates do). In that situation, the less-earning partner would be left with pennies on the dollar in their personal bucket. Not so for their high-earning "roomie." That partner would be living high on the hog thanks to a stuffed personal bucket. Fifty-fifty like that might work for roommates, but it certainly doesn't work for lifemates.

MAKE YOUR PLAN

Now that you've got the gist of buckets, it's time to customize your setup, guided as follows. One couple might take a few hours to work through each stage; another pair might need several days. Aim for what works best for you both, focusing especially on what best ensures you're practicing good communication, patience, and compassion. Tired, overwhelmed, overloaded people are lousy communicators—especially when they try to sort out money matters.

1. DETERMINE SHARED GOALS

Sketch out your shared goals. These goals should have a financial connection. Goals might directly address a money-related aspiration (buy a boat) or they might be a lifestyle goal that's contingent on finances (retire by fifty-five). Use this stage of the conversation to practice your communication around money.

Opt for productive questions along these lines:

- What do we want our future to look like?
- How soon do we want to get there?
- Do we want to be debt-free? If yes, in how many years? *0 debt.*
- Do we want to own a house? A farm? A second home? How soon? *not right away . . .*
- When do we want to retire?
- Do we want kids? How soon? How many? *1-2*

2. TRADE FINANCIAL AFFIDAVITS

As you review your fiancé(e)'s affidavit, keep in mind that while it is important to know figures, the habits, behaviors, and patterns revealed by the numbers are just as important—if not more so.

Some questions to ask could include:

- "I see $14,000 in savings, is that an emergency fund? Do you have a retirement fund, or is that what the $14,000 is for?"
- "How do you like to pay your credit cards? Is the balance I see new or is it carried over? What do you use your cards for? How are your interest percentages on those?"
- "How many years are left on your car loan? What do you pay monthly?"
- "Can you count on annual raises? Or commission?"

3. WALK YOUR PARTNER THROUGH YOUR FINANCIAL AFFIDAVIT AND ANSWER THEIR QUESTIONS

There is a story behind every financial affidavit, and in this step, each partner gives context to theirs. This is each person's chance to turn an accounting document into a personal narrative. One might have drawn from a college fund their parents set up to cover tuition, while the other put themselves through school and now has related loan debt. One might have a trust fund and the other might have had a job since they were thirteen. For the best conversation, you'll fare best by making this a judgment-free zone and sticking with productive statements. You are where you are, and it's time to move forward here and now—together.

4. DETERMINE THE FINANCIAL BEST PRACTICES YOU WANT TO INCORPORATE INTO YOUR MARRIAGE

A best practice is an agreed-upon procedure that works best for a team or company. A marriage's financial best practices include things like:

- how and when household bills will be paid;
- how to track your money flow (with an app, a Google Sheet, or otherwise);
- how your three buckets will flow; and
- the percentage breakdown of each spouse's contribution to the buckets.

Best practices indicate the terms for your financial merger. These guardrails are elemental to harvest the full benefits of *The Prenup Prescription*. Include them in a prenup, and you have transformed a static paper document into a daily blueprint for your marriage, one that strengthens it minute-to-minute.

To hash out your household's best practices, share what practices are mission-critical for you, and have your partner do the same. If you're hesitant, remember, you're a professional, which means you've had to advocate for yourself in your career. The voice you've developed there has served you well. If this isn't familiar turf for you on the homefront, it's time to bring your personal voice up to your professional speed. If, on the other hand, you fall into the steamroller category, remember this isn't the office, you're not competing with your spouse for a top spot, and neither of you is the boss of the other. You're equals. And now's the time for each of you to learn to communicate as such. **In a marriage, you *must* develop your voice as an equal partner as well as honor the voice of your spouse.**

Best-practice guardrails can, and should, evolve as trust grows and times change. We did this with expenses at my firm. Being Mr. Spreadsheet, I have always known to the penny what I owe, what I have, and what's coming in or going out. (You try graduating from Emory and then Harvard Law solely with scholarships and student loans; that kind of debt will turn even the chillest person into a financial hawk!) Opening an office felt like I was hemorrhaging money, first with gushing, arterial bleeds then with a never-ending stream of little pinpricks.

So I told everyone I needed to personally approve all expenditures. In time, once we had built trust and established frugality as an operating principle, I eased up. We set a $100 spending cap check-in, and I've been perfectly happy not to talk about office supplies since. If we had done the reverse, things wouldn't be so rosy. When you start off willy-nilly with no spending boundaries but then add them in, the change comes off as a punitive clampdown. Not only does the change put everyone on pins and needles, but it also generates resentment. Every time a co-worker would see that five-dollar desktop stapler they had to get permission to buy, a little more fuel would get added to the pile. The divorce clients I see come in with resentments like these, which in time flamed into the big problems that brought them to my door for an extinguisher.

The things you determine in this conversation are not necessarily things that will go into your final prenup, but to get the full benefit of *The Prenup Prescription*—to use these steps to build your marriage's foundation—establishing best practices around money now is essential.

5. ESTABLISH A SPENDING CAP CHECK-IN

A spending cap is the amount of money at which you'd like to be consulted before your partner makes a purchase or investment using an account you share. Set a household spending cap that's based on the reality of your financial health, based on your goals (rather than impulsive buys), and based on each of your comfort levels.

anything that isn't a bill or previously agreed on investment contribution needs to be discussed if coming from our shared account.

6. APPOINT A CHIEF FINANCIAL OFFICER AND A CHAIR OF YOUR HOUSEHOLD BOARD; CREATE A MASTER LIST OUTLINING EACH OFFICER'S ROLE AND DUTIES, AND DETERMINE YOUR BOARD'S BEST PRACTICES

I prefer to check off expenses that come out of the Thomas Household accounts and bills that have been paid—in real time. That means daily. I've been told by a lot of people that this makes me...unusual. So be it. Twenty years of experience tracking my finances daily has made me the perfect candidate for CFO of the Thomas Household Financial Board. That's the position I hold; my wife is, of course, the board's Chair.

For our board, we've outlined some baseline best practices, which include: *I like this!*

- full access to each other's financial accounts, passwords, and financial management tools;
- open invitations to any meetings with financial advisors; and
- annual meetings to update one another, review our numbers and strategies, and plan new goals.

Honestly, we treat the Thomas Household Annual Board Meeting as legit as if it were any other corporation board we served. (Yes, I referred to the Thomas Household as a company. Because—are you sick of hearing this yet?—all legal marriages represent a legal financial merger, which, in my mind, renders them into an entity of their own.)

WHY CALL IT A CFO?

Just like in a true company, your household CFO manages finances and reports on the group's financial status at regularly scheduled board meetings. Formalizing a spouse's role like this may seem silly, but it's actually a healthy way to consider their appointment. A household CFO is not "in charge" of the household money; rather, they are in service to the company and to the household. They are accountable and answerable to their other board member and shareholder.

7. GATHER YOUR PLANS INTO A WRITTEN DOCUMENT, REVIEW, AMEND, AND FILE WITH YOUR FINANCIALS FROM STEP ONE

Once you've outlined your intentions, add it to your home prenup file. When you've completed Step Three, you'll take all the paperwork you've generated to a family law attorney who will convert the materials into the legal document that will become your prenup. Ask them if they see anything that you may want to rethink or consider. Know that they won't include overly granular elements or things that can't be relegated by law. They will, however, extrapolate those that can be upheld in court based on laws and their experience as a family law attorney in your state.

To generate the clauses you will include necessitates that you and your partner cover a lot of ground. That's intentional; to get the most out of *The Prenup Prescription*, it's critical to traverse that turf together. You're laying a solid marriage foundation built of fiscal bricks, using essential marriage tools—transparency, communication, fairness—as mortar.

WHAT IF I AM LOATHE TO $HARE THE REIN$?

Who wants to give up their financial independence after they've been autonomous for years? Pretty much no one. Who has anxiety over their own money matters, creating financial plans, rules, and organizational models? Pretty much everyone. Sharing those responsibilities won't be comfortable for anyone's first time out of the gate. But if you want to get married and stay married, this is the leap. That said, if you've worked this step thoroughly, you're going to land safely on terra firma.

CHAPTER SIX

Step Three: Plan for Your Future

Marriage Tool: Fairness

DETERMINING WHETHER SOMETHING OR SOMEONE IS ON this side or that side of the fair-unfair seesaw can be a minefield and an emotionally expensive undertaking. When it comes to marriage, though, I don't think "fair" requires a complicated definition. Fair is putting your marriage first. Fair is seeing your spouse as an equal. Fair is making choices in your marital finances that bolster teamwork, honor compromise, facilitate transparency, value equity, and foster both trust and security between you and your spouse.

Unfortunately, unless you have a prenup, marital law is set up so a couple has to agree on what's fair at the *end* of their marriage—precisely when they are guaranteed to be most at odds with one another. By the time I see a divorce client, they are to-the-gills fed up with their spouse and have next to no patience and/or grace to call upon as they slog their way through negotiations. Usually, their other half mirrors the same. Neither one usually has a clear, uncompromised mindset, in other words, the mindset needed to make the monumentally impactful, binding, and detailed calculations and agreements divorce necessitates.

Speaking of obvious things, couples always seem to be able to grasp the logic of alimony *before* getting married, like when I draft their prenup. That proves my point about couples being most fair during their engagement rather than after their vows. I continue to be amazed at how, by the time I am involved as a divorce attorney, the higher-earning spouse is so quick to devalue the personal and financial sacrifices of the spouse who ceased working to care for children, an elderly parent, or other dependent. I've heard these types say, "Well, I earned all that. Why do they get half of what *I* earned? I've been supporting them for years." I wonder if I'll ever stop being amazed at how such people can't recognize family contributions save for those earned outside the four walls of a home.

Daddy issues!

If, by some miracle, a person taps into a hidden reserve of fairness, they might tell their lawyer that they only want to do what's completely right by their spouse. They might tell their lawyer they want to be fair and generous. So the attorney drafts a magnanimous offer and sends it over to the other side.

Do you know what happens? Whether it's the lawyer, their client, or both, someone gets suspicious. They think the generous spouse must be hiding something. That it's got to be a trick. Because there's no way they can be putting an offer so seemingly fair and generous on the table unless it were a trick. And, because suspicion is powerfully contagious, the lawyer convinces their client they have to go for more. They reject the offer, which, in the end, had the opposite effect of its intention.

Things play out this way because divorcing spouses live in an emotional state that can render them unrecognizable to themselves, let alone to their soon-to-be-former spouse. Paranoia and fear power the roller coaster the two ride. Both jostle along, this one reaching for the brake and that one for the accelerator. This side files a motion, and that side files a response. Legal fees mount higher and higher and the ride plows on, fast-slow, start-stall, unfettered by timeframes and timelines. There are only two ways to get off: ride the coaster all the way to trial or give in to exactly whatever the other side wants. Neither option is pretty.

I'm a prenup evangelist because it doesn't have to be this way. But as an evangelist, I have to deliver the harsh truth alongside the path to salvation. Here it comes: **Right now, while you're engaged, you're poised to be the most fair you can ever be with your intended.** You read that correctly. During an engagement—not during a marriage—is when you and your beloved are most capable of being utterly fair to one another.

That's because, during an engagement, each person has:

- equal standing;
- equal stakes;
- equal bargaining power;
- equal freedom; and
- equal rights.

This makes it the prime time to address contingency plans. Fairly.

CONTINGENCY PLANS?

Step Three sets you up for "happily ever after," a state you can reach even if your marriage *doesn't* make it all the way to "till death do us part." Should your marriage end, a well-rendered prenup is the best path anyone has to a turnkey divorce. Ask someone who's been through a divorce without one if their case was turnkey. No? Ask them if a turnkey prenup would have made the process and the aftermath better. Thought so. The secret to as seamless a split as possible lies in contingency plans, which are plans made to care for yourself and your spouse, along with others impacted by your marriage. While most everyone homes in on the most dire prenup contingency of them all—divorce settlements—there are many others to address that have absolutely nothing to do with splitting up. Let's start with those.

Marital contingencies affect a couple's future during their marriage or when one spouse outlives their mate. They facilitate goals and dreams. For example, good health insurance can beget affordable medical treatment which—with a stork tossed in—could, fingers crossed, beget a healthy, bouncing baby. A well-managed retirement account can determine retirement age and dictate the quality of that retirement. Life insurance can assure a person's mate and dependents that they will be cared for should its policyholder die.

Marital contingencies can address things like:

- marriage counseling;
- health insurance;
- trusts;
- retirement accounts;
- savings accounts;
- advance healthcare directives;
- life insurance; and
- wills.

On the flip side, divorce contingencies establish the plans that a couple will enact should they divorce. They are plans made to facilitate the dissolution of a marriage. Ideally, putting divorce contingencies into a prenup allows a person to say to an attorney, "Here's the prenup, here are my notes and financials for the divorce settlement (based on the prenup), and now...let's get this over with." Attorneys can even lift settlement clauses verbatim from a good prenup and paste them into a divorce agreement. A shortcut like that adds up to fewer hours billed to both parties; in other words, prenups equal insurance against bad divorces.

Divorce contingencies can include:

- divorce filing terms;
- family, couples, and individual counseling;
- settlement terms (distribution of assets and debts, and alimony);
- mediation clauses; to avoid going to court
- arbitration clauses; and
- trigger clauses.

MARITAL CONTINGENCIES

Use big-picture conversations to nail down the marital contingencies you want to add to the blueprint of your prenup. While some are no-brainers ("We'll maintain insurance policies"), others should be talked out, even if they don't ultimately get included in your prenup.

Consider questions along these lines:

- What are your expectations around us working?
- If we have children, how will we raise them while earning a living?
- What will our household policy be if/when a family member or friend needs money? No (unless from our "mine" accounts)

- Are we going to/not going to help our parents as they age? Define what "help" means.

No. • Would we ever have anyone move into the house with us?

It may be easy to say no to having another adult live in your house now, but you might change your tune when one—or both—of your moms needs moderate caretaking, and they've lived so long their savings accounts are anemic...or empty. Besides learning where each other stands on specific matters, these kinds of asks should point out concerns one or both of you will want to address. Addressing these concerns in a prenup generates trust, security, and reassurance—powerful peacemakers, all.

AREAS TO ADDRESS

Most marital contingencies will only be top-level referenced in your prenup. That means the clauses that make it into the legal document will simply state one or both parties agreed to do this or that. If you get too detailed, you run the risk of turning your prenup into five different contracts, and there's only so much the document can do. (Your best bet for discerning what should make the cut is to rely on the expertise of a family law attorney.)

Possible marital contingencies to put into your prenup include:

Estate Planning

- We agree to establish who has power of attorney over our estate.
- We agree to maintain updated individual legal wills.
- We agree to list the other as a beneficiary in our will.

Financial Practices

- ☆ We agree to make any personal loans (like those for family and friends) out of our respective individual accounts, not our shared accounts. *Yes!*
- We agree to share discretionary money equally should one of us leave the workforce. *Maybe if for child rearing but not if quit/fired.*
- ☆ We agree to skim 5 percent from each of our annual take-home incomes and put those funds aside for a shared, agreed-upon purpose (such as a vacation fund, a baby fund, etc.). *Yes TBD on % though*
- We agree that the premarital owner of 123 Prenup Lane will pay all of the property's capital home improvements and that both of us will split utilities and other "renter" expenses fifty-fifty.

Assets and Debts

- We agree that how we have titled assets at the time of marriage (and will title assets throughout our marriage) determines ownership.
- ☆ We agree each of us is responsible for our own student loan payments.
- We agree to a 60/40 percent split of the value of the home at 123 Prenup Lane, in favor of its premarital owner.
- ☆ We agree to pay off joint and individual credit cards monthly and not carry balances.

Life Insurance

- We agree to maintain life insurance policies.
- We agree to list our spouse as our life insurance beneficiary.

- We agree to increase the death benefit in our life insurance policies by $250,000 each time we become parents of a child.

Counseling

N/A?
maybe?

- We agree to attend at least two sessions of couples counseling, should either spouse trigger this clause.
- We agree to enact the above compulsory "trigger" clause no more than four times a year.
- We agree to enter rehab or otherwise seek treatment if either of us experiences legal consequences for an alcohol- or drug-related incident.

Religion

N/A

- We agree to [baptize, christen, mitzvah, etc.] our children.
- We agree to raise our children in the [fill-in-the-blank] faith.
- We agree to allow our children to choose their own religion.

NONCOMPLIANCE AND TRIGGER CLAUSES

What happens when one spouse does not abide by contingencies? Let's say a couple with a prenup files for divorce. Their agreement has a noncompliance clause that is connected to their settlement terms. If all contingencies had remained unbroken by both parties, they would divide their marital estate fifty-fifty. If one or more contingencies had been broken, the marital estate would be divided into a sixty-forty allocation of assets to the detriment of the non-compliant spouse.

That's how trigger clauses work. But contingency noncompliance doesn't have to result in divorce. Instead, noncompliance could initially trigger marriage counseling sessions with the aim of righting the ship. However, if chronic noncompliance becomes a dealbreaker (remember, financial dynamics equal relationship dynamics) and the pair does split up, the pre-set, revised settlement percentages would take effect.

PARADOX OF POWER

Believe it or not, the most powerful aspect of putting a contingency into a prenup isn't its triggering consequence. Rather, a contingency's power stems from having it—and your shared commitment to it—spelled out in black and white.

Maybe you get married and you have a honeymoon conversation that ends with you agreeing that neither one will give friends and family handouts from your pooled account. Then, oops, six years down the road, you do just that without having consulted your spouse. Your other half finds out, balks, and says, "Hold up, remember when we were on our cruise right after the wedding and we said we weren't gonna loan money to family members or friends?"

Perhaps you sincerely forgot, perhaps you don't recall ever having established such a ground rule, or perhaps you each had different perceptions of what "loan" meant. Welcome to Fightville, population two. On the flip side, put a loan clause in a prenup, and there's no ambiguity for either of you.

DIVORCE CONTINGENCIES

I see divorce contingencies as one of the most romantic things imaginable. I'm not kidding. Divorce contingencies are legal pledges that state no matter what comes, you want your partner to be treated fairly and to be taken care of. They also represent a reflection of your individual self-worth. When an affianced partner voices what they need in a divorce contingency, they declare themselves to be worthy of respect, fairness, and care. I include divorce contingency clauses in the following categories, among others.

COUNSELING

Some of the worst divorces I've seen amount to one spouse springing a divorce on their mate. I'm talking about someone getting served divorce papers when they did not even know their partner had determined the marriage was over. To avoid such misery, I like to include a prenup clause that says prior to either spouse initiating a divorce, each must attend a minimum of four (or however many) counseling sessions together. Clauses like that can also state that whoever presses the counseling button will give the other written notification the clause has been triggered, and that sessions must begin within ninety days of such notice. Counseling can just as soon be a marriage contingency (therapy sought in order to better an ongoing marriage) as it can be a divorce contingency (therapy sought in order to help couples process an ending marriage). During the latter, a therapist helps the couple resolve issues in the hopes of making their breakup less acrimonious.

CONTESTED DIVORCES

If either or both parties challenge any part of a divorce agreement, they are said to contest the divorce. In a contested divorce, there are a few paths forward. The goal of each is to determine the divorce settlement, custody and visitation, child support, and so forth.

Mediation

I recommend a prenup clause that requires mediation prior to either spouse filing a divorce petition directly with their county clerk of court office. (Some states require mediation before a divorce can go to trial.) In mediation, a trained, third-party mediator (usually a lawyer) guides the two parties through negotiations in order to settle disputes. The couple chooses a mediator, who earns an hourly fee—typically several hundred dollars. I include deadlines and payment terms in mediation clauses. For example, I'll note mediation must take place within thirty days of the couple's last counseling session, and that both spouses will pay equal portions of the mediator's total bill.

Settlement terms reached in mediation are drafted into a formal legal agreement and co-signed by both parties in the divorce. The plaintiff or the plaintiff's attorney then files the paperwork with the local county clerk of court's office. Once processed, the agreement (called a divorce settlement) gets assigned to a judge who then reviews it. When the couple's court date arrives, both parties and their counsel appear before the judge for a brief (twenty minutes or less, usually) confirmation of their identities, current marital status, intent to divorce, and endorsement of the signed agreement. The judge next notes their approval of the settlement and verbally pronounces them divorced. After that, they sign an official, one-page divorce decree, which is the legal order stating the couple has been freed from their marital contract. This decree is paired with the signed and notarized original divorce settlement and is filed at the clerk of court's office in the county where it was issued. The time between mediation and a final decree tends to be several months.

Some states require couples to attend mediation before they can move on to either arbitration or a court trial. That's because mediation serves several purposes. First, it unclogs the family court system, which speeds up the divorce process for all those seeking to dissolve their marriages; there are only so many lawyers, judges, clerks, courtrooms, and more available in any one geographic area. Second, it provides divorcing couples a forum in which to reach an agreement before things get really ugly and really expensive.

Arbitration

also agree

If you can't come to an agreement via mediation, you can either pursue arbitration or opt for a courtroom trial. As in mediation, in arbitration, both parties select the go-between, an arbiter (usually an attorney), who is paid hourly. The arbiter, however, is unlike a mediator in that they don't play a role in helping both parties reach a compromise. Rather, they are akin to a judge in that they hear each side's case and then make a binding ruling (called an order) that spells out the couple's full divorce agreement. Arbitration is like a mini-trial, except it's privately conducted, and the parties have a hand in its guardrails.

For instance, they might say arbitration is not to last longer than a day and must commence within ninety days of a failed mediation. One of the main benefits of arbitration is that its proceedings take place outside of a public courtroom, which helps if children and/or the parties' livelihoods need the protection such privacy affords. A decree and settlement terms reached through arbitration are, however, filed with the clerk of court, which makes them part of the public record. The other chief advantage of arbitration is speed. Court trials can take close to a year or more to begin, and they can be dragged out innumerable ways once they commence. Opt for arbitration and you minimize the financial, emotional, and logistical toll divorce proceedings undoubtedly have on all those involved.

SETTLEMENTS

A settlement is an enforceable legal agreement that resolves any dispute or negotiation between two or more parties. It includes clauses (directives) that outline the terms (specific actions). A divorce settlement captures what you and your spouse will do with respect to the dissolution of your marriage. Settlement documents reflect a couple's division of assets and debts, alimony terms (if there are any), custody terms, and child support (should they share any children).

Settlements can be generated outside formal negotiations like mediation and arbitration, and outside court trials, but no matter the origin, they must be legally sound. The safest bet to ensure the agreement is legal is to have an attorney draft it.

Alimony

Alimony is the term for money paid from one spouse to another after a divorce. Normally, the higher-earning and/or otherwise financially better-off spouse pays alimony to the lesser-earning spouse. The most common reason people come to me for a prenup is usually to take alimony off the table.

I tell these folks to hit the pause button and think it through. Let's say you intend on having children, I'll posit. Do you plan for one parent to stay at home to raise the kids? If not and you both continue to work, which one of you plans to lessen your workload (or step into a less demanding position) to accommodate the inevitable needs of children? Also, should any of your children need unforeseen, hands-on care, be it short- or long-term, who of you will trade work hours for parenting?

I explain that if one spouse were to leave the workforce due to childcare, they would lose earnings and otherwise stall their career in general. Should a couple in that situation get divorced, and the primary caregiving parent re-enter the workforce, at best they would be out of date in their field of expertise. At worst, their knowledge base would be obsolete. In either case, their earning power inevitably would be nowhere near the level it had been, nor anywhere near that of their continuously employed peers. They would have lost years of salary, raises, bonuses, and more. And, as is always the case with children, their expenses would have gone up and up and up. Given all that, I tell them, wouldn't it only be fair to give the primary caregiving parent a financial transition period—via alimony—post-divorce?

Calculating Alimony

I keep prenups—and certainly prenup math—as dummy-proof as possible. To calculate the duration and amount of alimony for a spouse who traded in their career for child-rearing, I use a ratio like this:

Alimony duration = X years ÷ months of alimony for every Y years ÷ months a spouse was out of the workforce

Alimony amount = 15% × The difference between the couple's individual gross annual income

Gross annual income is determined by averaging each spouse's last two tax returns. The payment cycle varies; you might break an annual alimony determination into twelve equal monthly payments to be paid on the first day of every month. Further, you could also add a stipulation that alimony ceases should the recipient spouse get remarried or begin to live (romantically) with someone else. *yes*

Another alimony stipulation might be a cap on the maximum

annual income one can earn and still receive spousal support. For example, you could stipulate if either spouse were to make more than $50,000/at the time of a divorce/ they would not receive alimony. Common sense factors in here. If one spouse makes, say, $500,000, and the other is making $200,000, an income cap is irrelevant because anyone earning either sum would clearly be able to cover expenses without outside help.

Assets and Debts

Few things can rile anyone up more than dividing up or being told to share "their" stuff. It zips people right back to the sandbox and brings out their inner three-year-old. (Besides "No!" my preschooler's favorite word is "Mine!") I don't know about you, but the decisions I made at that age do not line up with those I make today.

That's where a prenup's asset and division contingencies come in. Here's one example of how such contingencies can direct a divorcing couple as they divide their marital estate.

The division clauses would state they will:

- sell all assets that, prior to seeking a divorce, were not designated (by title or prenup clause) as being individually owned by either spouse;
- hire an appraiser to determine an asset's value or sale price should the couple disagree on the same; and
- determine the choice of appraiser thusly: one spouse shares a list of three experts, and the other spouse picks one person out of the nominees.

Just like they do with alimony, my prenup clients typically come with preset ideas for splitting property. They usually outline something like this: whatever each came into the marriage with, each keeps; whatever they built or acquired during the marriage is split fifty-fifty. Sure, that's fair enough, but it's also asset division in a vacuum, and it doesn't account for appreciation, among other things/

Designating Asset Ownership

In Chapter Two I mentioned that after you are married, there is no such thing as "my money" in the eyes of the law. We need to talk about that a little more precisely and clarify who owns what before a marriage, during a marriage, and after a marriage.

Why? Too many people are under the false impression that if a married couple doesn't mix accounts, swap payments, or share titles, this thing 100 percent belongs to that person, and that thing 100 percent belongs to the other. I can't repeat it often enough: the law says when you marry someone—without a prenup that indicates otherwise—you have agreed that come what may after the vows, be that debt, a new asset, or new equity in (and appreciation of) a premarital asset, counts as marital property.

I indicate a couple's intentions of ownership with property titles:

- If the intent is to own something jointly, both spouses' names will go on the title, indicating fifty-fifty ownership.
- If the intent is for only one of them to own something, only their name will appear on its title, indicating 100 percent ownership.
- If something remains titled in one person's name, but the couple's intent is to share it (like a house or a retirement account), each partner's percentage of ownership will be specified.

In addition, I include a blanket clause that states titles indicate ownership. The blanket clause also mentions title style applies to property both before the marriage, as well as after it has commenced. To give assets belts and suspenders—make the intention ultra-clear and super secure—we also list out each considered asset in the prenup.

Often there's appreciation and increased equity to account for. That gets most tangled when one partner owns a house before the marriage (making it a separate, premarital asset) and the other partner moves in after the wedding. If the new "roomie" contributes to the value of the property—via mortgage payments, home improvements, etc.—the appreciation and equity increase in the home since the marriage can be seen by a court as shared (marital) value. Rather than ride blind over how a judge may or may not rule, I like to untangle and neatly tie up such loose ends. The easiest way to show you how to sort it out is with an example.

CASE STUDY: HOW THE HECK WOULD WE DIVIDE A HOUSE I OWNED BEFORE WE GOT HITCHED?

Hang in there, this is going to get detailed, but you can handle it—I promise. Here's the overview: Jan bought a house with a mortgage loan before marrying Lexi. After they married, the house remained titled in Jan's name, but each of them contributed toward the mortgage.

In their prenup, they had indicated their intent for Jan to get two different shares of the equity and appreciation of the home. One share would be based on her premarital ownership stake in the property. The second would be Jan's half of their outlined fifty-fifty split in the house's appreciation and equity since the wedding. Lexi would get one share, half of their outlined fifty-fifty split in the house's appreciation and equity since the wedding.

After their wedding, each spouse contributed equally toward the mortgage. Five years into the marriage, the house's market value was $50,000 over what Jan had originally paid for it.

Here's the breakdown of how it would be divided if they divorced in that fifth year.

By the Numbers

Jan owns 40 percent of the house as her separate property. (No matter what happens, she retains that 40 percent of the house as her separate property.)

Five years into marriage, the house is now worth $150,000.

The bank owns $40,000 of the house.

Jan owns $60,000 of the total value of the house as her separate property. ($150,000 house's total current worth × 40 percent of Jan's separately-owned portion of the house = $60,000)

Jan and Lexi own $50,000 of that together as marital property. ($150,000 house total current worth – [$60,000 Jan's separately owned portion – $40,000 the bank's portion] = $50,000)

Each owns a $25,000 portion of the marital property. ($50,000 total current value of marital property value ÷ 2 = $25,000 each)

Jan owns $85,000 of the house. ($60,000 Jan's separately owned portion + $25,000 portion of the marital property = $85,000)

Lexi owns $25,000 of the house.

Infidelity Clauses and Getting Carried Away by What-Ifs

I did a prenup consultation recently for a would-be client who made way, way more money than their fiancé. The man in my office said he wanted a prenup with a gold-digger clause that would be triggered by infidelity. (A clause like this states that should a spouse cheat, they forfeit their rights to alimony, property, and so on. They are enforceable in some but not all states.) I told him—as I tell other clients with such requests—that if they continued on that punitive path, they were dooming themselves to one mess of a marriage.

In real life, if a person actually steps into an actual rabbit hole, there's a good chance they will break their leg. Suffice it to say it's best to stay away from rabbit holes, and the same generally goes for punitive provisions related to marriage.

"I need you to understand how the negotiation on this is going to go," I told the guy who was clearly obsessing over what-ifs. "I know your partner's attorney, and I can guarantee you if you start putting in provisions with built-in punishments, this process is going to go really, really long. Really, really long equals lots and lots of money, which equals lots and lots of acrimony. *true ...* If everyone getting married tried to dream up every bad thing the other person could do and then attempted to account for each bad thing in a prenup, there'd be no end. Some things wouldn't even fall under a prenup's jurisdiction.

"As someone who's been in this business a very long time, I have to tell you this: if a cheating spouse is intolerable to you, your best remedy is to leave the marriage."

I never saw the man again.

The thought that your future spouse might not be faithful is not pleasant, to say the least. I understand that no one wants to be cheated on, but there are several reasons I advise skipping mention of it in prenups. (Postnups are, however, a little different. See why in the Appendix.) As I see it, if a person has gotten to the point where they're going to step out of their marriage and have an extramarital relationship, they are not thinking of the consequences. First, they don't think they're going to get caught. And second, they're certainly not making decisions based on percentages in a prenup. So if an infidelity clause is not preventative, then it's solely punitive.

Let's walk through a punitive cheater clause from a practical stance. To begin with, how are you going to define cheating in your prenup? How specific are you going to get? What if you and your spouse build up $4 million in assets over the course of a thirty-year marriage? During those three decades, you each had one fling. Only one of you got caught—say, you—and now, all of a sudden, your share of the marital estate drops from $2 million to $1 million...or less. For thirty years, you faithfully contributed to create that $4 million estate, and then you make a mistake that erases those decades of work.

Some people—especially those who don't have years of marriage behind them—may answer that yes indeed, it is completely fair; it's black and white. Me? I'm not so sure. Maybe it's all the broken marriages I've seen, but rarely have I come across a divorce that's 100 percent black and white, good spouse versus bad spouse. From what I've seen, fairness—the cornerstone of Step Three—often hides out in the gray areas.

For example, what if one partner has been the victim of recurring physical spousal abuse? Maybe in a moment of weakness, they sought comfort from someone else. If their prenup includes a cheater clause, they would end up with less money and the abuser would get the lion's share. Switching gears, consider if one spouse becomes addicted to heroin, meth, pills, porn, alcohol, or whatever, and they go to prison for years on end on related charges. After a decade on their own, the spouse on "the outside" has a brief affair. If the convicted spouse finds out and files for divorce, would it be fair for their other half to lose all claims to the couple's marital estate? The estate that they kept nurturing on their own, years after their mate was incarcerated?

I get why people are scared of commitment these days. I get why it's tough to trust each other. And I get that for those of us used to controlling our careers, embracing a big, impactful variable can be uncomfortable and even frightening. But trying to account for every bad action your spouse could do during your marriage is a pattern of thinking that does neither of you any good. Plus, after you've opened Pandora's box of what-if clauses it's all too tempting to only address one behavior. That's the nature of what-if poison. Soon you'll be trying to weigh cheating against drug addiction against physical violence against everything awful that someone can do. Trouble can find you easily enough on its own; why go courting it?

CHAPTER SEVEN

Tact, Timing, and Talk

MY ELDEST SISTER IS A BIG-TIME, SUCCESSFUL JOURNALIST, and she tends to have more financial assets than the person she's dating. Being the prenup evangelist I am, I long ago converted my family, so it's a given that anyone in our crew who slips on an engagement ring next makes an appointment with their lawyer. Ah, romance! Because my sisters and I have seen our parents work as a true team, financial and otherwise, for decades upon decades, and since we weren't raised to be shy, broaching the subject of a prenup to a sweetheart is no big deal. And it certainly is not for my big sister. Add that she's literally a pro at asking difficult questions without coming off as confrontational, and her singular brand of directness married with diplomacy makes her the perfect person to advise those of you who might be dreading the prenup talk.

So I asked her. How would she talk prenups with a fiancé, particularly one who might be prenup-averse? Of course, she laughed and whip-fast replied that she'd read this book in front of him—in bed, on a car trip, on the sofa, etc. "Beyond that," I prodded.

"Simple," she said. "I'd tell him I want to talk about how we'll set up our finances when we're married. Then, either in that same conversation or in a related one, I'd mention how I'd heard a prenup can fit in as a basic element of our financial plans. I'd bring up your gospel, of course—dropping a 'My little brother the lawyer says...' never hurts." (Those at home *not* related to me can use the lead-ins I list later in this chapter.)

She said as she and her partner continued the conversation, she'd tell him she wanted to get advice from a financial professional—someone who could review what they came up with and/or give them even more direction. Of course, in this case, that financial advisor would be a prenup lawyer. The more pragmatically you approach it, she said, the better.

My wife is cut from the same cloth as my sisters (go figure), but she comes to the topic of prenups as a divorcée. Maybe your fiancé(e) is in that same boat but hasn't considered one for the two of you. Perhaps Christina's take might be of interest to them. She says our prenup enables her to make choices based on what is good for Team Thomas, versus making defensive, fear-based choices that stem from her past experience. She says she's all about our custom prenup because she has zero interest in finding herself in a second financial nightmare. Instead, our rock-solid legal prenup gives her an overarching sense of security. She says she doesn't worry about prioritizing family—caring for our daughter or other family members—over her career. She also tells me it is easier for her to stomach the hours I put into work because she knows whatever I earn is 50 percent hers. And she knows every dollar I earn flows straight into our "Ours" bucket. Further, she has all-access at all times to the apps that organize our finances. With a click of a button, she can see precisely what she would walk away with if she left me right then and there. That's what financial transparency in a marriage means. "And transparency," she says, "feels good."

HOW DO YOU SEE PRENUPS?

I just did a prenup for someone who just graduated from law school; at twenty-five, she's the youngest client I've ever had. She's marrying her high school sweetheart, and told me coming to my office was a no-brainer for both of them. "We have always been pro-prenup," she said. "*Always.*"

A lot of couples—especially those who were born when the divorce rate peaked in the eighties and nineties and those entering their second marriage—fall into the same camp as that young pair. These types are typically terrified of *not* having a prenup. Why? Because they don't have the luxury of thinking *Divorce can't happen to me*. For them, getting a prenup makes "taking the leap" more palatable. For them, a prenup means they won't have to jump blindly into financial darkness. It means they won't be merging their corporation without a contract.

Obviously not everyone counts themselves among the pro-prenup crowd. There are plenty of reasons for this, including our culture. Raised on the Disney side of life, some prefer to revel in their role of prince or princess right up to the fairy tale finale—their big day. In the movies, by the time the credits roll, everything's wrapped up nicely in a big bow, no loose ends, no tarnished crowns. These people are guided by a neon pink "All you need is love" light. It's a choice to spend an engagement this way, living in a world of pretty wedding Pinterest boards, engagement ring emojis, "bride" sashes, and congratulatory posts.

But you're smarter than that. And so is any partner who is worth marrying.

Hard conversations now make for easier ones down the line. And easy conversations now make for hard ones later. Avoidance of the truth is a habit you have to break now before you get married. Talking about money with your spouse should not be akin to teeth pulling. It's something to practice and get comfortable doing. That said, as someone who has to read the courtroom each time I try a case, tact and timing are vital when you break the ice around typically tough subjects. Truth reigns, yes, but it doesn't have to do so with a heavy hand. Here are some tips to be the most productive when you get down to the discussion.

BROACH THE SUBJECT ASAP

I would rather people talk about prenups *before* they get engaged. I admit that I'm not exactly typical, though, and that most people don't enter a marriage as a lawyer, let alone as a lawyer marrying another lawyer, like Christina and I. If you do first broach the subject when you are already engaged, get the ball rolling as far ahead of your wedding as possible. Going to a family law attorney a month before a wedding could work in a pinch for financially organized couples, if they were already sold on the concept altogether. The target time (besides ASAP) should fall when both partners still have enough time to find and secure good representation and work through the process I've prescribed on these pages. As you choose that cutoff, ask yourselves how long you require to work the steps of *The Prenup Prescription*, most likely while you plan the wedding and work, too.

PAY ATTENTION TO WARNING SIGNS

The way one spouse treats their finances is going to impact the other. If you bring up finances, and your partner loses it, curses you, storms out, and slams the door, that is something better known now than later. In a healthy partnership, no one should object to disclosing their assets and debts. And healthy couples also agree it's advisable and normal to talk about budgets, how to cover expenses, and how to set up accounts. If your fiancé(e) gets defensive or evades transparency surrounding their income, their debts, or their assets, take it as a flashing danger sign. Any hints of that nature should be addressed now, before you head down the aisle. Premarital couples' counseling can sometimes get to the root of the matter. If it doesn't, look for another important sign: the exit.

BE POSITIVE

Creating a prescribed prenup is a two-person foundation-building exercise for your marriage. As such, aim for a positive conversation, not a confrontation or power grab. Here's an example of a positive opening to the subject: "I want to make sure we're doing everything we possibly can to make our marriage succeed. I read that when a married couple is transparent about their money and outlines how they will conduct their finances before they get married, they tend to have fewer arguments after they are married..." (Wow, I sound like a lawyer. Obviously you should put your own spin on that script.)

LAY A PATH FOR FUTURE PROBLEM-SOLVING

Getting on the same page about your finances is not optional. If you and/or your partner could benefit by enlisting outside help to do so, be it professional (therapists, financial advisors, or religious figures) or personal (trusted mentors, friends, or family), get it. There isn't anything wrong with seeking help before you marry, and doing so won't doom your marriage any more than getting a prenup will. In fact, normalizing the use of third-party expertise as a logjam solution forges a productive path for you to follow when future stalemates crop up in your relationship.

BREAK THE ICE

Appropriate any and all ideas from *The Prenup Prescription* that could facilitate your prenup adventure. Here are some specific conversation starters you might try:

"I just read a guide on how to have a successful marriage, and it's centered on finances..."

"I think it's a good idea for us to have some sort of marital budget—and a joint bank account. What do you think? We could use the shared account to pay for things that relate to both of us..."

"What sort of big-ticket 'musts' are on your bucket list? I'd love to set up some sort of budget where we save money so we can make that sort of stuff happen—for both of us..."

"I've been wondering how we would sort out who pays what when we're married. I've never merged finances with someone else. I'd love to integrate some house rules around how we'll tackle money..."

"You know that coffee machine I just bought? Did I tell you it was $500? How would you feel if I bought something like that when we're married, without checking in with you? As for me, it would be really, *really* tough if you did that, at least if you paid for it out of our joint account..."

Conclusion

BECOMING A PRENUP EVANGELIST WAS NEVER A BUSINESS idea. I simply didn't want to suffer through what I saw my clients suffer through, and I didn't want my family or friends to suffer, either. And I hate—always have, always will—that so many people, engaged or married, are in the dark about marital finances and the laws that govern marriage in general.

When I realized that financial fingerprints were all over the relationship strife I witnessed in one nasty divorce after another, I thought I had solved the puzzle. But I hadn't. At that point, I believed all that was needed to make the peace was to enlighten clients about the legalities of marriage before they said "I do." Draft them a regular prenup with sound financial affidavits, division clauses, and spousal support details, and though they might get divorced, at least they wouldn't do it messily. It was only when I tried to write the prenup my wife and I would sign that I realized I had missed the bigger picture, and with it, a massive opportunity.

The way I handled my own money as a single person was my taken-for-granted default. But Christina and I don't share all the same defaults around money or in all other things, either—no one does. Still, we made it to marriage by being open with one another; owning up to our habits; and respectfully compromising based on what was best for each other. In other words, we let transparency, communication, and fairness drive our relationship bus, and those three principles still fuel it. When I awoke to the full potential of a prenup—the role it could play in the health of a marriage, not just in its demise—and folded transparency, communication, and fairness into ours, I found the security and hope I needed to propose. The document we signed became our roadmap and, even though it sits in a drawer collecting dust, we operate according to it each day.

In the divorce cases I have encountered, most couples didn't make those critical principles the guiding lights of their marriage. Perhaps things started out in the right direction but weren't maintained. Perhaps they rocked one principle, but not all. Undoubtedly they hadn't spelled the principles out in print or made adherence to them legally binding. These folks aren't unique. Scores of us don't communicate authentically with others, let alone our mates. We usually avoid true intimacy—I'm talking stripped-down, embarrassingly honest transparency—as much as possible. And without those pillars, achieving fairness in a relationship is impossible for anyone.

But there is a solution. If you sort out where each other truly stands (Step One), build a structure for interacting financially (Step Two), and plan for the inevitable (Step Three) you will be living in the solution. You will be following the prescription and practicing each of its marriage tools. And while I'm definitely not a fortune teller, I can promise that following *The Prenup Prescription* will give you the keys to, at best, a healthy marriage, and, at worst, as short and inexpensive a divorce as possible. Heck, even if you opt for a committed relationship rather than a formal marriage, you and your mate can still follow the prescription and benefit.

And it's not just the two participating people who reap the rewards. When you and your partner talk openly, honestly, and respectfully about financial matters (and about how money factors into the inner workings of your relationship), you inherently point the way for those around you to follow suit. And you pass on an updated, modern financial marital dynamic to your children. The only ones who might not be thrilled or benefit are those divorce lawyers who prefer profit over people.

Here's what I hope happens next. I hope you get your own prenup (duh). I hope you put it in a drawer. I hope you enjoy the peace of mind that its guaranteed security brings. And then, most of all, I hope that you never, ever have to open that drawer and look at your prenup again. But, if you must, I want you to know that with it in hand, everything will be okay.

Appendix

Timeline of Marriage Laws

THE FORTHCOMING TIMELINE COULD ALSO BE REFERRED to as, "Legal Examples That Spell Out Just How Much Marriage Was Devoid of Romance—and Otherwise Generally Sucked for Women—Until Mere Moments Ago When Considered in the Course of Thousands of Years of Recorded History."

It could also be referred to as, "The Kinds of Things Men Have Proclaimed, Ruled, and Put into Law Concerning Women, Love, and Marriage Through the Centuries, Which Is to Say, Marital Laws Are Based on Whacked Ideas and Traditions, Which Underscores the Imperative to Read—and Thus, Only Knowingly Accept—De Facto Marital Laws before Reciting Your Vows..."

Or you could just consider this timeline as yet one more way I beg you to act in your best interest by grabbing the reins of your marital destiny with a prenup—the only thing that's guaranteed to supersede the sort of insanity you're about to read.

CIRCA 2350 BC
OLDEST RECORDED MARRIAGE

As far as surviving written records go, the oldest official marriage takes place between a man and a woman in Mesopotamia. Today, those lands are recognized as Iraq, Kuwait, Turkey, and Syria.

This record shows that marriage as a formal, legal undertaking has been around for some 6,400 years. Love-match marriage? That only became normalized in the last hundred years, which accounts for only 1.6 percent of all the years marriage has been recorded.

1754 BC
THE CODE OF HAMMURABI

"If a man wish to separate from a woman who has borne him children, or from his wife who has borne him children: then he shall give that wife her dowry, and a part of the usufruct of field, garden, and property, so that she can rear her children. When she has brought up her children, a portion of all that is given to the children, equal as that of one son, shall be given to her. She may then marry the man of her heart."

—LAW 137 UNDER HAMMURABI, THE
SIXTH KING OF BABYLON

Law 137 mandated child support, alimony, and asset division for a mother—whether a wife or a lover—abandoned by the father of her children. He was to return her dowry and give her fertile land to grow crops, which provided sustenance. When she had reared their children to adulthood, she was to return a portion of the land to him and was then free to marry anew.

AD 1184-6

"Love can have no place between husband and wife."

—ANDREAS CAPELLANUS, "THE ART OF COURTLY LOVE"

This twelfth-century French priest served Marie of France (daughter of King Louis VII) after she was married off to Henry I, the Count of Champagne. Bibliophile Marie commissioned "André le Chaplain" to put his thoughts into writing, and he penned several books, essays, and more. Later in "The Art of Courtly Love," André made clear where "courtly love" was acceptable: it belonged solely between a husband and his lover or a wife and her paramour.

CIRCA AD 1380-1444
SIENNA, ITALY

"Exercise a little restraint and treat your wives with as much mercy as you would, your hens and pigs."

—FATHER BERNARD

Believe it or not, in his day, Father B was seen as a progressive among Catholics. Today people might recognize him more easily by his sanctified name: Saint Bernard of Sienna.

1736

"The husband cannot be guilty of rape committed by himself upon his lawful wife, for, by their mutual matrimonial consent and contract, the wife hath given herself up in this kind unto her husband which she cannot retract."

—SIR MATTHEW HALE, *HISTORY OF THE PLEAS OF THE CROWN*

English judge Sir Matthew's treatise proclaimed spousal rape didn't exist as a crime. His reasoning was that when a woman trades marriage vows with a man, she has entered a contractual obligation, one that gives him the right to have intercourse with her under all circumstances, until death do they part. His words informed centuries of marital law.

1765

"The very being of the woman is suspended during the marriage, or at least is incorporated and consolidated into that of the husband; under whose wing, protection, and cover, she performs every thing..."

—WILLIAM BLACKSTONE, *COMMENTARIES ON THE LAWS OF ENGLAND* VOL. 1

Referred to as the British Coverture Law, this edict means that, legally speaking, upon becoming a man's wife, she ceases to exist as a separate, legally recognized individual. She has been acquired and duly appropriated by her husband.

1839

Mississippi passes its so-called Married Women's Property Act, becoming the first in the nation to give a Mrs. the right to own property in her own name.

At first pass, this act may seem awfully ahead of the times for an antebellum-era Southern state—it wasn't until 1900 that married women could own their own property nationally—but dig into the details and it might read differently. The law stemmed from a case in which a Chickasaw woman sued to keep the enslaved people her father had bequeathed to her out of the hands of debt collectors. Her (white) husband owed a lot of money and wanted to sell them to pay off his debts. When the judge ruled in the woman's favor, thereafter, any property owned by a Mississippi wife could not be seized based on the actions of her husband. Married men found a workaround, though. In the decades following the passage of the law, a husband would shield his own property from collection by listing it in his wife's name.

1868

"[The] decision is not that the husband has the right to whip his wife much or little; but that we will not interfere with family government in trifling cases. We will no more interfere where the husband whips the wife than where the wife whips the husband; and yet we would hardly be supposed to hold that a wife has a right to whip her husband. We will not inflict upon society the greater evil of raising the curtain upon domestic privacy, to punish the lesser evil of trifling violence..."

—*STATE V. A.B. RHODES*, NORTH CAROLINA

While North Carolina courts and lawmakers didn't condone beating one's spouse, they also wouldn't establish as much in rulings or laws. Why? Because what happened in one's home was, apparently, no one else's business. It was first in 1979 that the state passed its Domestic Violence Act, which outlawed abuse in the home, be the parties married or not. However, it may be worth noting that 1979 was the same year the Tar Heel legislators passed another gem that became known as the "right to finish" law. It stated if a person had consented to have sex but revoked their consent once the act was underway, the aggressor's actions couldn't be classified as rape. In 2019, North Carolina's governor signed the Freedom From Abuse Act, which repealed that absurdity, along with the one that said if a person has rendered themselves too "incapacitated" to resist sex, their consent was not needed.

1871

Alabama becomes the first state to rescind the legal right of men to beat their wives.

Wife beating was common and accepted in Alabama in the 1800s. Six years after the Civil War ended, a case involving a formerly enslaved husband and wife went to trial. At that time, married Black couples had only recently achieved legal recognition and rights. In a move many historians cite as retaliatory, the judge convicted the husband in this case, creating a precedent that could be used to break up Black families. (White husbands continued to beat their wives with no recourse.)

No matter how you interpret the 1871 ruling, it's worth knowing Alabama lawmakers (narrowly) removed the prohibition of interracial marriages first in 2000. The same proposition was (narrowly) voted down in 1996.

1874

"In order to preserve the sanctity of the domestic circle, the Courts will not listen to trivial complaints. If no permanent injury has been inflicted, nor malice, cruelty nor dangerous violence shown by the husband, it is better to draw the curtain, shut out the public gaze, and leave the parties to forget and forgive. No general rule can be applied, but each case must depend upon the circumstances surrounding it."

—*STATE V. OLIVER*, NORTH CAROLINA

For a century after this ruling, lawyers successfully used this precedent to protect husbands from being prosecuted for spousal rape.

1882

"Any person who shall brutally assault and beat his wife shall be guilty of a misdemeanor, and upon presentment and conviction thereof by any court of competent jurisdiction, shall be sentenced to be whipped, not exceeding 40 lashes, or be imprisoned for a term not exceeding one year, or both, in the discretion of the court..."[3]

Flogging had an on-again-off-again history in Maryland. In 1808, it was banned from use against whites—not enslaved people—as an official punishment. In 1882, formal whipping returned to the state, but with a stipulation. There was only one qualifier: it must be as punishment for wife beating. (It was reasoned that imprisoning a wife-beater deprived his family of economic support, so there needed to be an alternative penalty.) While the last such beating officially took place in 1938, it was only taken off the books in 1952.

1920

"The right of citizens of the United States to vote shall not be denied or abridged by the United States or by any State on account of sex."

—NINETEENTH AMENDMENT TO THE US CONSTITUTION

For an engaged person on the verge of being governed by state marital law, it's noteworthy that the Nineteenth Amendment was passed just one hundred years ago.

---

3   "Whipping Post—Lest We Forget," *The Baltimore Sun*, July 23, 1972.

1922

"Be it enacted by the Senate and House of Representatives of the United States of America in Congress assembled, That the right of any woman to become a naturalized citizen of the United States shall not be denied or abridged because of her sex or because she is a married woman."

—THE CABLE ACT

When women got the right to vote in 1920 as a result of the Nineteenth Amendment, suffragettes next tackled citizenship. Congress ratified The Cable Act in 1922; it established a married woman's citizenship as her own. For fifteen years prior, a separate bill had dictated that American citizens (women) who married non-naturalized men (non-US citizens) assumed their nationalities. No matter where she lived, on American soil or abroad, when a wife lost her nationality, she had no American liberties or protections.

1945

A California judge dismissed the murder charges against a husband for killing his wife. Using the Equal Protection clause in the Fourteenth Amendment, the judge established spousal abuse laws to be unconstitutional because they discriminated against men. Following that logic, he dismissed the case.

To be fair, this case was an aberration, an outlier. But it's worth noting because it illustrates the unpredictable nature of a legal system like ours. You never know how lawyers will wield laws and precedents, nor how judges will rule.

2022

"Sexual battery, as defined in Section 16-3-651(h), when accom-
plished through use of aggravated force, defined as the use or the
threat of use of a weapon or the use or threat of use of physical
force or physical violence of a high and aggravated nature, by
one spouse against the other spouse if they are living together,
constitutes the felony of spousal sexual battery and, upon con-
viction, a person must be imprisoned not more than ten years."
—SEXUAL BATTERY CODE, SOUTH CAROLINA CODE OF LAWS

At press time, this statute stands without any motions to amend
or rescind it. The inherent problem lies in the phrase "aggravated
force." Such language forces a jury and judge to determine how
aggravated and how forceful a case of sexual battery is. If they
don't see a case as aggravated and forceful, it wasn't criminal.
Further, the code creates a giant loophole. If a victimized spouse
were rendered incapable (i.e., drugged or drunk) of resisting or
recollecting a battery, does it count? The first spousal rape law
in America was only passed in 1975 in Nebraska. Up until then,
a man could rape his wife with no legal consequences.

1993

"A person may not be prosecuted under this Article if the victim
is the person's legal spouse at the time of the commission of the
alleged rape or sexual offense unless the parties are living sep-
arate and apart."

—NORTH CAROLINA LAW CODE

Protecting a husband's right to sexually assault his wife is a
longstanding tradition in Western law. In 1993, North Carolina lawmakers revised the state's code to read, "A person may

be prosecuted under this Article whether or not the victim is the person's legal spouse at the time of the commission of the alleged rape or sexual offense." With those edits, North Carolina became the last state to outlaw spousal rape. (For reference, three months earlier Oklahoma legislators revised their spousal rape laws.)

Timeline of Divorce Laws

LET'S SWITCH GEARS AND FOCUS NOW ON DIVORCE LAWS. The following timeline could also be referred to as, "Examples That Illustrate How, Until What Amounts to Essentially Mere Moments Ago, Marriage and Divorce Laws Have Been Perversely, Intentionally, and Legally Constructed to Subjugate Women, and Strip Them of Basic Rights."

Or it could also be referred to as, "State Marriage and Divorce Laws Have Only Very Recently Been Modernized—and Then Only Sparingly—Which Underscores the Imperative to Read—and Thus, Only Knowingly Accept—De Facto Marital Laws before Reciting Your Vows."

1739

The first divorce in the American colonies was granted in Massachusetts. The grounds? Bigamy on the part of the husband.

1849

"Such misconduct as permanently destroys the happiness of the petitioner and defeats the purpose of the marriage relation..."

— CONNECTICUT STATE LAW

Connecticut courts added what amounts to an "unhappy marriage" clause to a handful of grounds for divorce. The New England state also allowed divorces to be sought by either spouse.

1940–1970S

Several states make it possible for fathers to get custody of their children and/or for wives to pay their ex-husbands alimony.

Until the first half of the twentieth century, state laws commonly gave mothers automatic custody of children unless they were insane or an addict. These revised laws represent a flip of historical norms wherein a woman equals the default caretaker of children, and thus, is chiefly valued for producing offspring. Under these new laws, women are considered capable of supporting their ex-husbands and are not simply assumed to be the best at raising children. That said, while the laws technically began treating women as equal opportunity earners (i.e., capable of paying alimony) and men as fully capable caretakers, judges still commonly reach verdicts based on biases that are millennia-old.

1966

New York deems domestic violence grounds for a wife to divorce her husband.

However, in order to be granted such a divorce, the wife must prove that she had been beaten "a sufficient number of times." That stipulation demanded that, before she was legally allowed out of her abusive marriage, she must prove her allegations in public. Further, given the times, a woman in this situation was most likely still living with her husband. It does not take a legal savant to realize the flaws in this law.

1969

"Dissolution of the marriage or legal separation of the parties may be based on either of the following grounds, which shall be pleaded generally:

(a) Irreconcilable differences, which have caused the irremediable breakdown of the marriage.

(b) Incurable insanity."

— CALIFORNIA FAMILY LAW ACT

Then-Californian Governor Ronald Reagan signed the country's first "no-fault" divorce into law, which established irreconcilable differences as grounds for the dissolution of a marriage. This law's passage became one of the biggest leaps forward in the fight for women's rights in America. But they weren't the only winners. Part of its appeal to male lawmakers was that it helped ex-husbands keep more money in their pockets. Find the story of how it came to be in "How Divorce Became No One's Fault (and Why It Needs to Stay That Way)," later in this Appendix section.

1970S

Battered women shelters are established for the first time throughout the country.

The advent of shelters represented a cultural shift in the abuse of women. During the seventies, such abuse changed from being a common and widely accepted private matter—especially in marriage—to being recognized publicly as unacceptable and problematic. Laws always lag behind cultural shifts, but eventually, they reflect such changes should they be widely accepted by the majority of society for a long period of time.

1975

Up until 1975 a man could rape his wife with no legal consequences in all fifty states. Beginning in 1975, a handful of states began passing laws prohibiting what was called "spousal rape."

During the 1960s several state legislatures had actually passed laws to make rape permissible not only for wives but also for live-in girlfriends, as a response to the decade's free-loving culture that mainstreamed shacking up. If women were going to skip marriage, local governments were going to treat those who lived with their lovers the same as they did wives. The consequence of these laws was that if a woman lived with her boyfriend, her choice was legally equivalent to her consent to grant him sex on demand, under any circumstances—the same rights husbands enjoyed. In 1975, the scant early laws that criminalized spousal rape drew ire and attack as being anti-religious. Why? Because such laws went against the religious origins and intentions of marriage.

1980S

Consent slowly begins to factor into marital sexual relations.

Today we (almost) take it for granted that rape is defined as a lack of consent by one of the parties engaging in sexual intercourse. But considering marriage has been around for thousands of years, the idea that a wife doesn't give unconditional, eternal sexual consent to her husband is a completely modern concept.

1984

A New York court rules raping your wife, estranged or not, is a crime.

In 1980, New York officials ordered an abusive husband to stay away from his wife. In 1981, he tricked her into meeting him in a motel room, where he trapped, beat, and raped her—all in front of their two-year-old son. While he didn't deny what he'd done, he did contest that what he had done was criminal. (It's worth noting that no husband had ever been convicted of marital rape at that time in New York. Ever. Perhaps that was the source of his and his attorney's gall.) His lawyer argued the rape amounted to personal business between a man and his wife, and thus, the court should stay out of it. They were still married, after all, and a 1978 law might have said raping one's *estranged* wife was illegal, but they weren't formally separated by law, and there was nothing on the books that said forced, non-consensual sex between a man and his wife could be prosecuted as rape.

A trial court agreed with the defendant and dismissed the charges against him. That first ruling was overturned on appeal, which led to his conviction. The second court looked at the law and determined that since he was legally ordered to stay away from her, they *were* legally estranged—the only loophole in the 1978 law. By 1984, the husband had appealed his way to the state's highest court, the New York Court of Appeals, where its justices supported his conviction on moral grounds. Their ruling established that raping one's wife, estranged or not, would thereafter count as rape in New York.

1993

All fifty states have a law banning marital rape.

The banning of spousal rape was another huge turning point for married women. By giving them legal dominion over sexual intercourse, it was legally established that wives were not property, nor were they owned by their husbands. All legal vestiges of wives being considered property were not eliminated with the adoption of these laws.

2016

For her husband to be prosecuted for spousal rape, a wife in South Carolina must file a report with law enforcement within thirty days of the incident or her claim is invalidated.

2022

In Virginia, someone who rapes their spouse can be ordered to undergo counseling rather than face criminal charges.

2010

New York becomes the last state to legalize no-fault divorce.

Marriage Anachronisms

LAST NAMES AND MAIDEN NAMES

For most of America's history, we've been a patrilineal society—
we indicate family kinship based on male lineage. Children carry
the last name of their father and when women marry, they most
often give up their "maiden name." Calling a woman's last name
at birth her maiden name is a holdover from the Middle Ages
when the word "maiden" indicated virginity. While a woman
was her father's charge, she was expected to remain a virgin,
and thus, bore his last name—her name as a maiden. Marriages
were validated by consummation, so a newly deflowered woman
took on the name of her husband to indicate her changed sexual
status. Her name change also marked the moment when she
ceased to exist as her own legal entity. Today, when an officiant
introduces Mr. & Mrs. Same Last Name to wedding ceremony
guests, as seen through a historic lens, it represents a public
proclamation that the wife has officially been absorbed into the
groom's clan. A written wedding announcement introducing a
couple as Mr. & Mrs. Same Last Name, a married woman who

legally changes her name to her husband's, and a newlywed wife who adopts a new monogram...each of these actions is rooted in old marital laws and customs.

VEILS, WHITE GOWNS, AND FATHERS GIVING AWAY DAUGHTERS

Most wedding guests view a dad walking his daughter down a wedding aisle as a sweet tearjerker. Sentimentality, however, didn't birth the tradition. The process of a father walking his daughter-bride into a ceremony and then unveiling her has historically represented a father's presentation and ownership transfer of a maiden daughter as property. The word "unveiling" refers to this custom, a holdover from the times when a groom might not have laid eyes on his bride until they traded vows. A veil emphasized the vulnerability of maidens, and it's been said they also ensured a wary husband-to-be couldn't back out based on his would-be wife's looks. (Along those lines, it's also been said that a father remained by their daughter's side in case her groom might bolt.) As for the gown said daughter is wearing? In Western cultures, it's white to symbolize purity (i.e., virginity), a color that became customary after Queen Victoria donned a white gown for her 1840 wedding.

"HE'S A GOOD PROVIDER...SHE'S GOT CHILDBIRTHING HIPS"

For centuries, the success of a marriage match was gauged by ensuring financial success and healthy offspring. Even today, a husband (or prospective husband) might be viewed in those terms. Whether said for bragging rights, as comforting comments, or possibly as justification for tolerating less desirable traits, "He's got a good job," and "He's a good provider," remain common in our lexicon. And if you've ever heard a woman described as having "child-birthing hips," by old standards, like a horse with a good set of teeth, it meant she's a worthwhile investment. After all, good birthing hips sauntered hand-in-hand with fertility, right? Together the combo practically guaranteed that a man's name, legacy, and holdings would be passed on to his plentiful, hardy offspring.

"HAPPY MARRIAGE"

English philosopher John Locke wrote that happiness was elemental for true liberty. Thomas Jefferson liked Locke's take so much he enshrined the pursuit of happiness as an inalienable right in the United States Constitution. It was—quite literally—a revolutionary idea. Weaving this right to happiness into America's core governing principles made it intrinsic to our culture. Embracing the right to happiness, over time young couples extended its reach; surely, if one was entitled to a life of happiness, that meant they were also entitled to a love-match marriage. Justified as such, they turned down "practical" marriages arranged by their parents—the historical norm—and instead pursued those of their own choosing. As for what constitutes a happy marriage today? Under the happiness umbrella, it's one that stems from two people being hit by Cupid's arrow and is measured on a postnuptial basis by how lovingly the spouses feel for one another.

NO MONEY FOR WIVES WHO CHEAT

While most current laws stop short of defining married women as their husband's property, ghosts of that perception remain on the books. In Georgia (as of press time), if a wife cheats, she has forfeited her right to alimony and she has also put her share of the marital estate at risk. Punitive "moral" mandates like these are leftovers of English Common Law, which stated a wife's vows equal her consent to grant her husband exclusive use of her body.

A Postnup P.S.

I COULD HAVE BECOME A POSTNUP EVANGELIST, CALLED myself "Mr. Postnup," and written a book called *The Postnup Prescription*. But I didn't. If a postnup is exactly the same as a prenup, which it is, legally speaking, why push prenups instead?[4] Because timing is everything.

Postnups get signed after a couple's wedding, and while a postnup is better than no such marital contract at all, prenups are the better choice. Always. That's because timing equals leverage. Until a happy couple trades vows and signs their license, the partner who earns less holds precisely the same bargaining chip as the one who earns more: The right to say "I do" or "I don't." But as soon as these two make things official, that leverage disappears faster than a wedding band packs up at cutoff o'clock.

That said, there are several reasons couples seek a postnup. Here are the most common reasons I've encountered.

---

4   As of press time, postnups are legal in every state but Iowa and Ohio. Laws regarding postnups (like most other laws) continue to evolve, so rather than make a misstep thanks to an outdated online post, visit a family law attorney for the most current facts and specifics.

REASON ONE: TIMING

Amid the countdown to the wedding, some couples simply can't make it to the attorney's office to sign and notarize their otherwise fully baked prenup. If the signing deadline passes like that for one of my prenup clients, I edit the document as needed, and...voila! It becomes a postnup. Others get a postnup well into a marriage, and I've even done them in the lead-up to a divorce. Typically the timeframe doesn't impact the agreement being enforceable. In one case, I worked with a couple who knew their marriage was on the rocks. The partner who had hired me shared that if they ultimately broke up, each spouse wanted the fastest and most inexpensive divorce possible. In other words, they wanted a postnup as insurance against a messy divorce. Spelling out settlement terms and details while they were still civil actually helped them honor their marriage and even their vows.

REASON TWO: SILVER BULLET

Sometimes two people seek a postnup in an attempt to save their marriage. I once represented a wife in just that scenario. She had caught her husband in an affair; he wanted to reconcile. They sought to rebuild their relationship, and to do so, my client said she needed a legally sound financial safety net. She was only asking for what made sense. Years prior, they had decided she would leave her lucrative job as a surgeon to raise their children full-time. His affair had pulled the curtain on how economically insecure and professionally vulnerable she was. Surgery isn't a field that's simple to resume after a prolonged absence. And, should she update her skillset and knowledge base and return to the OR, she would never get back years of missed raises, promotions, and opportunities. The way they saw it, a postnup could include financial makegoods to replace what she'd given up. To that end, they asked me to include a trigger clause stating if the marriage ended due to his infidelity, he would pay her a specific (and generous) alimony for life. Moreover, she would walk away with 60 percent of their marital assets. I later learned they did, in fact, divorce. I bet that postnup came in handy.

REASON THREE: ASSETS

Postnups can also rewire a married couple's financial relationship. A couple in this camp may have an otherwise good personal relationship, but something in their marital finances is malfunctioning and it's causing tension. Usually, the culprit is a big asset, like a house.

The issues tend to stem from the homeownership minefield outlined in earlier chapters:

- A person owns a house before marriage.
- They get married and their spouse moves in.
- The house title remains the same.
- The title-holding person continues to pay the mortgage.
- Their spouse covers a separate, comparable shared expense in exchange.

"We thought that this setup was going to work for us," a client once told me, "and it is most definitely not."

"Not only is it not working, it's causing fights," added their partner.

Rather than simply changing the title to the house, they wanted to untangle the knot of who pays what, who owns what (and how much), and on. So we devised a postnup that established a financial blueprint for all things money matters, from asset ownership to household expense responsibilities, best practices, contingencies, and on.

✴ REASON FOUR: BUSINESS

When a spouse becomes an entrepreneur well into a marriage, a postnup can provide security for both that person and their other half. I did one such contract for a perfectly happy couple. Their sole concern revolved around the wife's new startup. She was a scientist and had invented a truly revolutionary treatment for cancer patients. She patented her groundbreaking process and created a small company related to it. By the time I talked to the pair, the company had taken on investors, and it had the interest of a major pharmaceutical group. Joint ownership of patents makes for a mess, and making her husband a major shareholder at that stage was complicated with respect to the investors' ownership rights. The husband, who was also a medical researcher, had funded most of the business during R&D when his wife quit her lab job to focus on what she eventually patented. He had also paid their bills for several years during that time. While things were on track for the company to take off, the timeframe for its payout was indeterminate. They both had decades of experience in their field and knew how these things can go. Would the megacorp buy the company in a year? Twenty years? The wife wanted to ensure her husband that he would get his fair share of any spoils it might generate. To do so, I created a postnup that stated should a payout come—whether during the marriage or after the marriage—he would get half of her windfall.

✈ REASON FIVE: EMBRYOS

A postnup can clarify frozen embryo ownership and create legally binding actions around them in the event of divorce. For example, one biological parent could cede their parental rights to the other on the condition they would not be responsible for the support or custody of any subsequent child. Another option is that a couple would agree to keep the embryos frozen in perpetuity according to a specified storage plan, including its cost. Alternatively, a postnup could also indicate their mutual consent to donate or discard the embryos.

How Divorce Became No One's Fault (and Why It Needs to Stay That Way)

"ON SEPTEMBER 5, 1969, WITH A STROKE OF HIS PEN, CAL-
ifornia governor Ronald Reagan wiped out the moral basis for
marriage in America." So wrote the author of a law review paper
published in the summer of 1969 in *The American Journal of
Citizenship*. Yes, the same man who went on to become the
fortieth president of the United States was once blamed by millions for the downfall of marriage in our country. These same
detractors also warned of its inevitable consequence: a society of
wayward women, deadbeat dads, and caught-in-the-middle kids.

Today, most married couples who split cite "irreconcilable
differences" as their legal grounds to do so; most probably don't
know this option was made possible by Reagan's passage of California's no-fault divorce law. Here's how that snowball turned
into an avalanche that liberated women throughout the country
while providing "faulty" husbands their best chance yet to hold
on to their money, property, and reputations.

It's 1965, California. Family courts are overrun and backed up beyond belief. Advisors have alerted Democratic Governor Edmond "Pat" Brown, who forms a commission to suss out the logjam. The team determines the clog stems from a few sources, one of which is divorce. Governor Brown tells investigators to home in on divorce and suggests they find efficiencies related to it alone.

Getting a divorce in early 1960s California is predicated on a limited number of legal grounds (reasons): one of the spouses must be proven in court to be an addict, mentally ill, an adulterer, or an abuser. Each petition for divorce requires a hearing to present evidence that supports the presence of the fault. After each side pleads their case, a judge then decides to grant the divorce...or not. If one spouse is found to be at fault, the judge can then supersede the state's community property laws that otherwise mandate a fifty-fifty split of the marital estate. The magistrate can, thus, determine shares (and alimony) through their own subjective lens. In addition, alimony is assessed by how "at fault" a husband was for wrecking the marriage.

The commission sees these divorce hearings as the court system's chief hang-up and offers up this fix: whittle a marriage's exit options down to a single ground that doesn't require a trial, one like "irreconcilable differences." Do that, they tell Governor Brown, and getting a divorce becomes little more than a rubber-stamp formality. Each spouse gets assigned a court date and appears before a judge.

"Is the marriage irretrievably broken?" the judge asks whoever filed for divorce.

"Yes," the filing spouse answers.

"Is there any hope of reconciliation?" the judge asks them.

"No," both spouses reply.

The judge then runs the numbers to establish alimony, using the newly proposed, standard formula that now considers only the duration of the marriage and a wife's earning ability. From there, they outline the equally divided divorce settlement, and then down comes the gavel. Liberated, the wife's privacy (and possibly her safety) is protected while the husband's share of the estate (and possibly his reputation) remains intact.

To recap, the "breakdown of marriage in America" was due to a West Coast judicial efficiency put in motion by latter-day California governor Jerry Brown's dad. But is that how it was sold to the public? Of course not. By 1969, Ronald Reagan had taken over as governor of California. He positioned the proposed change as being in the best interest of caught-in-the-middle kids, abused wives, and unhappy husbands. (A former movie star, Reagan was not only a one-time Democrat who converted to the Republican Party, he was also divorced and remarried.) But it's unlikely that was the pitch given behind closed doors.

I've always been a big believer in economic power as a force for change. Like it or not, it almost always trumps the hope that people will own up to their actions and elect to do the right thing. When it came to cultivating support for no-fault among California lawmakers and powerbrokers, money definitely talked loud and clear to those with Y chromosomes. In the end, no-fault divorces caught fire chiefly because they led to what amounted to a financial windfall for at-fault men. When "irreconcilable differences" went into effect, how a married couple's assets were divided could no longer be resolved based on who was virtuous and who wasn't. When the irreconcilable difference movement was positioned in terms of men's wallets, Reagan was able to secure Republican co-sponsors of the bill and the support needed to see it into law.

As Reagan signed "no-fault" into law, he spoke of its lofty benefits. "I believe it is a step toward removing the acrimony and bitterness between a couple that is harmful," he said, "not only to their children but also to society as a whole." Nary a peep about court system efficiency or settlements. No wonder he was called The Great Communicator.

Initially, opponents continued to criticize the law and still labeled it an "easy out" to one of the oldest, most sacred, and most widespread of human institutions. This camp cited high rates of poverty in single-parent homes, an explosion in the divorce rate, and the troubles of the real victims of no-fault divorce—children. They argued if you took away no-fault divorce, couples would be forced to work through their problems. Intact families would lead to healthy, stable children. (Since then, research shows children are actually better off with two happy, conflict-free households versus one with domestic strife, violence, and so on.) The law not only held, paired with community property laws alongside alimony that are based on need rather than merit, but it also stands to this day.

The rest of the country caught the no-fault divorce bug, too. New York became the last state to adopt it in 2010.[5] In time, the community property approach to asset division has fallen out of favor, and, as of press time, only nine states follow it. The

---

5   Of course, while irreconcilable differences is the blanket ground for divorce, other grounds still exist, and vary from state to state. When I represent a client who is divorcing a particularly nefarious person, someone who has done some real lowdown, dirty deeds, I will sometimes include Georgia's additional grounds—adultery, cruel treatment, and desertion—in the formal filing just to have those on public record. As a strategy, it sends a warning to the opposing party: do they really want all of this to play out in court? And personally, it's a way to stand up— publicly—for someone who has been treated so wrongly.

remaining forty-one states have codified equitable division.[6] Equitable division—a more nuanced and subjective approach to asset division—puts judges back on the bench determining what constitutes each spouse's "fair" share of the marital estate. Yet again, they might listen to tales of cheating, cruelty, and addiction, alongside narratives around who served as the breadwinner and who reared the children. Courts are clogged again, and the newest valve release? In some states, it's a mandate making mediation a prerequisite for a trial or arbitration. Thus, the circle goes round and round.

---

6   An equitable division of property means a fair division of that property. "Fair" is subjective to the individual judge, and doesn't always add up to a fifty-fifty split. The only time a marital estate is authentically divided in half is when the case occurs in a so-called "community property" state. Today, only nine states remain as community property states. The others fall into the equitable division camp.

Scare-You-Straight Cautionary Tales

NOTHING TELLS THE STORY LIKE A TRUE-LIFE EXAMPLE. And after being a divorce attorney for some fifteen years, I've seen countless soul-crushing lessons play out among my clients. In the spirit of *Scared Straight* (and all its offshoots) here come a few case profiles to make you run, not walk, to a reputable family law office for a legal, enforceable, and well-thought-out prenup.

Among other unpleasantries, these true stories illustrate:

- how bad legal counsel can render you penniless;
- how finances can be weaponized when a marriage (without a prenup) goes downhill;
- how ironclad prenups can be—even in the most egregious of circumstances;
- how merely a draft of a trigger-clause postnup can send the message a wayward spouse finally hears.

WHAT REALLY BAD LEGAL ADVICE LOOKS LIKE

Oftentimes, a person doesn't realize their marital contract—be that a prenup, postnup, divorce agreement, or otherwise—is a bad one, until it gets tested with a legal challenge. (That's why I am a broken record about using sound legal expertise to draft yours.) Here is a case of a man who came to me with a decade-old divorce settlement agreement that he'd just realized was really, really bad.

When it was first written, his daughter was three years old. She was now sixteen. The agreement had the following terms:

- Both parties agreed to a fifty-fifty split of the cost of their child's first car. Each was to contribute at least $25,000 toward the cost.
- Both parties agreed to a fifty-fifty split of their child's college education costs for five years, capped at whatever the cost of attending Brown University was when said daughter came of age. (The parents were Brown alumni; for reference, in 2021, the school's annual cost was nearly $80,500.)
- Both parties agreed to a fifty-fifty split of their child's eventual wedding costs.

When this man and his ex signed their divorce settlement agreement, I'm sure they saw all these fifty-fifty clauses as perfectly fair. He told me his attorney had assured him it was the noble path to take. Ten years later, however, the mom had remarried, and her new spouse was off-the-charts rich. Private-jet rich. My would-be client, however, was not. Over the previous decade, the industry he had specialized in had been rendered obsolete. He pivoted into a new career in a new field, but starting over meant he made less—a lot less—than he had when he first signed the divorce agreement.

By the time he came my way, the couple's daughter was taking driver's ed and shopping for a college. A wedding wasn't on the horizon (he did, however, share that the teen was into scrapbooking and had already started one devoted to "My Big Day"). The man's ex had recently reached out to him to say it was pay time. He told me he wanted to be accountable, but how could he, given his financial reality? And, he asked, should he have to go halfsies given the stepdad's astronomical worth? "Sorry," I had to tell him, "but you're stuck."

If he tried to fight the settlement, any family law judge would throw up their hands. "I don't have the ability to change this," they'd say, "because no court ever had the ability to order you to do it in the first place." The moral: bad legal advice can sound good and still screw you over. It's one thing to make such provisions for children who are a year or two from cars, college, weddings, and so on. But to do so for a toddler? I would never suggest a client sign up for such specifics that far in advance. Because just as quickly and unexpectedly as a marriage can end, a person's fortunes can change.

MY "FIXER" PET PEEVES

There are two types of bad marital contracts that irritate the heck out of me because each can so easily be avoided. To begin with, virtually every DIY prenup or postnup that I've seen is unenforceable because the couple missed something—usually it's a painfully simple something—that a divorce lawyer would have flagged in a split second. One common oversight occurs with validating such documents. All marital contracts must be notarized, and some states require that witnesses sign the papers, too. All too often, I meet someone who teamed up with their spouse, wrote down their intentions, signed the agreement, and carried on thinking that was that. But it wasn't. Such a rudimentary agreement would get tossed out by any judge. In fact, no good lawyer would even let it get in front of a judge. These couples have to start their settlement agreements from scratch.

The second type of bad marital contract involves an attorney—the wrong kind of attorney. Apparently, a lot of people think marital contracts fall under an estate planning lawyer's purview. The problem is that when your attorney doesn't go to divorce court week after week to defend—or challenge—such contracts, they don't know the tried-and-true secrets of writing a foolproof document. And sometimes they don't know the bald-faced basics. I've actually seen marital contracts drafted by estate planning attorneys who join the ranks of the DIY couples who screw up signatories. Here in Georgia, your prenup must be signed by both parties and two witnesses before it can get properly notarized. Double witnesses are something of an anomaly in contract law, and, let me tell you, it's no fun explaining to a client that their Georgia prenup is no good due to signatory issues.

FOR RICHER AND POORER?

"I've been married to Gabrielle for almost twenty years," said a man I'd met who was going through divorce proceedings. "I've always been in charge of paying the bills—the mortgage, the kids' school tuition, utilities...you get the idea. I'd always paid out of our joint bank account, the one we set up when we first got married. That system worked fine until two years ago when we got into a huge—and I mean really huge—argument.

"After that," he continued, "my wife began direct-depositing her paychecks into a new personal account she opened—one I can't access. I know it sounds crazy now, but at first, I didn't say anything. I just kept paying for everything I could out of our 'joint' account, where I kept depositing my paychecks. Whenever I would get close to overdrawing, I'd tell her, and she'd transfer the exact amount needed into the joint account.

"After taxes, I make about $7,000 a month," he continued. "She's in the $9,000-range. For the past two years, she's given me about $1,000 a month for household expenses. I never challenged that or our new system.

"Then," he said, "last week, she filed for divorce."

Obviously, this couple had zero quality financial communication and a relationship that was neither fair nor transparent. The wife had to be flush with cash—I quickly guessed she had pocketed at least $24,000—while the husband was flat broke. Instead of asking what the heck their milestone argument was about, the question the rest of us should ask ourselves is: how can we avoid such a financial dynamic in our own marriages?

NO ONE CAN AFFORD TO BE BLINDED BY LOVE

Sometimes you take a case that you know is a long shot—even one that's beyond a long shot—because the client is adamant they would rather try to win than not try at all, odds be damned. I'm sharing one such story to exemplify how rock-solid prenups can be.

From all outward appearances, she had lived the good life with her ex. They met on a flight (her company owned the private jet), and soon after became inseparable. For a year, they traveled the globe, from one swanky hotspot to another. Because her job kept "interfering" with his wanderlust, he pressed her to walk away from her career. After all, he told her, he was going to pop the question soon. "Just when you will never expect it," he would tease. When her birthday approached, he brought up the clincher, "We have to get on that baby wagon, don't we...?"

She nodded. "All right then," he exclaimed, "time to go ring shopping!"

The next week, they were officially engaged. Two months later, friends and family joined them in an eleventh-century Tuscan castle overlooking the Tyrrhenian Sea to witness as they exchanged vows. The entourage included a cast of attendants, bridesmaids, and groomsmen that was thirty-souls strong. A couture wedding magazine had sent a crew of ten to photograph the festivities.

The night of their rehearsal dinner, her soon-to-be husband called her to their stateroom. She wondered if he was going to surprise her with more jewelry or some other sort of gift. I hope it has sapphires, she thought with a giggle.

When her fiancé opened the door, he gave her a quick kiss, and then stepped back, gesturing to a suited stranger she hadn't seen at first. "Meet Melanie," he said, "she works with Savannah's top law firm, and you two were in the same sorority. I hand-picked her just for you," he said, beaming. Melanie, he explained, had flown in an hour prior. "She's just here to help you understand what this means, in normal language," he said, handing his intended a thin stack of papers. "There's no way I would ever ask you to do something like this without having your own personal attorney," he said.

She thumbed through the papers. It was a contract. A prenup.

"If you don't sign..." he said, "Well—and I know how awful this sounds, I'm just so, so sorry—but my legal advisers tell me I simply can't go through with the wedding. I tried and tried to have them get the paperwork to us months ago, but they said they got sidetracked with that audit I told you about."

His bride could barely hear him; the ground felt like it had given way. He had never so much as hinted at a prenup. He'd always said after they were married, he would organize things so she would be taken care of, no matter what happened to him, no matter what happened to them. Plus, his finances were tied up in a lot of complicated holdings and trusts.

He wouldn't…she thought. As Melanie began to walk the bride through the contract, the groom slipped out of the room. After a bit, the lawyer also left. Through the champagne buzz her bridesmaids had kicked off hours earlier, she debated. A grandfather clock ticked loudly nearby. Without cessation, its hands moved forward, forward, forward. She took the antique as an omen, one intended to remind her that she couldn't afford to hit the snooze button on her biological clock anymore.

She signed.

Fast forward ten years later and there had never been the pitter-patter of little feet. He'd changed his mind about kids before they'd gotten to their first anniversary. But he wasn't youth-averse; in fact, he preferred spending time with nascent models, actors, and influencers more than with anyone else, which now included her. When she came home one evening and interrupted his raucous, heavily attended "slumber party," (which had spilled into their bedroom), she'd had enough. She told him they were done.

What allegedly happened the following week was, to say the least, unfortunate, and very unfortunately uncorroborated. After eating takeout he'd brought home for her and drinking a glass of wine he had poured for her, she said she blacked out. When she "came to" hours later, she said she was undressed and had been violated. She didn't go to the police because of the hundreds of reasons so many wives don't. She sent off a urine sample, however, and it showed traces of a common "date rape" drug. But collecting the sample on her own at home had compromised its chain of evidence. In other words, it was inadmissible.

That was the story the woman told me before she slid her prenup and his petition for divorce across my desk. "He had me served with this yesterday," she said.

I looked over the documents. She was to get $15,000 in alimony for every year of marriage. (This equaled what a full-time, hourly person working at minimum wage—$7.75 when they wed—would earn over twelve months.) In other words, she was to receive a little over $150,000, total. Other than her jewelry, a few closets worth of designer labels, and a smattering of antiques and artwork that were hers before they were married, that was it. She said she was auctioning off her belongings as soon as possible. This was unavoidable given he'd cut off her credit cards and locked her out of their accounts.

His financial declaration was among the papers. If I had to guess, I'd say he had handed it over so quickly because he was utterly confident in their prenup. His affidavit told me he was a one-percenter.

She said she didn't want much, just what she lost since she left her job. "Back salary," she explained, based on her annual earnings ten years prior. "When I earned $150,000 a year on my own," she said.

"I'm going to try to adopt," she added as I continued to review the file.

Before I could share any feedback, she blurted, "I know it's bad. I know I was stupid. But I was in love and thought I'd found 'The One.' Back then, I didn't meet many men who were interested in settling down—at least not ones that I clicked with, ones who were still single. I swear my biological clock was ticking so loud," she said, clearly embarrassed, "it covered up any ringing alarm bells I could have heard and it drowned out any warnings I could have been given. He promised me kids over and over, and I let that trump every doubt I had."

When she stopped talking, I shook my head. "The only possible option would be to get it overturned on one of the handful of grounds allowed in Georgia," I said. "That includes signing under duress; being denied legal representation; turning in a fraudulent affidavit; and displaying unconscionable favoritism toward one party.

"We can try to make the case that you signed under duress," I continued, "but 'duress' in legal circles isn't the same as pressure to act. Georgia judges equate duress to putting a gun to another person's head, shoving a pen in their hand, and then ordering them to sign or they'll pull the trigger. So we'd be mentioning duress primarily to show how he set you up, and to lay the foundation for the second charge—that the prenup's terms grossly favor him over you, and are, thus, unconscionable.

"But I have to tell you," I continued, "since Georgia's had prenup laws on the books, never has a single prenup been overturned based on unconscionable grounds. Not one. And it's truly awful, but alleged abuse isn't actually relevant to the enforceability of the agreement. 'Unconscionability' has to do with the terms of the agreement, not with the behavior of a spouse during the marriage.

"What about the rule that you can't sign a prenup too close to a wedding?" she offered.

"In Georgia," I explained, "so long as you have your own attorney—which you did—you can sign one right up to the actual wedding ceremony."

"What about me signing it in Italy, not here?" she tried.

"It has a clause stating it was written according to Georgia law, so those are the laws that apply to its enforceability."

She slumped in her chair.

* * *

The next year and a half I kept telling my client the odds were absolutely not in her favor. She always wanted to press on. The court day arrived, and she told a judge exactly what she shared with me. During her testimony, her ex shook his head and rolled his eyes.

After each party's case was made, the judge addressed my client directly. "I am so sorry," he said. "The decent thing to have done would have been for your husband to give you exactly what you've asked for. Unfortunately, the governing marital laws don't take decency into account.

"To overturn the prenup on grounds of duress," the judge continued, "he would have had to force and/or threaten you into signing at risk of bodily harm. Which he didn't.

"And as for him acting unconscionably," the judge frowned, "The terms of the agreement—not your husband's actions—are what I can rule on. Were the terms outrageous? Were they grossly, horrifically unfair? No. They are simply unfair. I'm afraid the prenuptial contract stands. I rule that you are both divorced under its terms. The plaintiff is to receive $150,000 in spousal support as well as her possessions and premarital assets as outlined."

We had known that whether a judge saw the prenup's terms as "unconscionable" was going to be entirely subjective. And we also knew that to rule in her favor would set a historical precedent for Georgia, something no judge takes lightly. Still, hearing the ruling aloud and publicly was so final, so cold. My client thanked me, and I haven't seen her since. I later heard she'd tried to sue him for abuse. Those charges didn't stick either.

Why tell her tale? To show you that case outcomes often have little to do with what we consider to be fair in the normal world. **And to remind you that no matter what, when it comes to the law, you can't afford to let love overrule your good sense.**

prenups.com

Made in the USA
Las Vegas, NV
11 March 2024

87068137R00100